How to Save

ESTATE AND
GIFT TAXES

How to Save

ESTATE AND
GIFT TAXES

BY

J.K. LASSER TAX INSTITUTE
AND RALPH WALLACE

NEW YORK · AMERICAN RESEARCH COUNCIL

LIBRARY OF CONGRESS CATALOG CARD NUMBER 55-5675

EIGHTH PRINTING, 1959

PRINTED IN THE UNITED STATES OF AMERICA BY

THE BOOK PRODUCTION COMPANY, INC.

Preface

The desire to achieve permanent financial security for your family is a natural incentive for the accumulation of property. Today, however, the ability to build up your estate is not enough to gain your objective; you must also guard against "tax lightning" that may strike in the form of estate taxes.

Unfortunately, many individuals think that estate taxes apply only to "millionaires," and that their own estate is not enough to be subject to the tax. But your estate may be much bigger—*for tax purposes*—than you realize, and one of the purposes of this book is to show you the scope of property that may be included for estate tax purposes.

But the Federal estate and gift tax laws are filled with opportunities for tax-wise savings. These permit you to select the method of conducting your affairs that will carry the smallest burden of tax. Their number and significance was substantially increased by the 1954 and 1958 tax laws, thus affording important new opportunities to save tax. But to get these benefits, you must make the right choices *before it is too late*.

The purpose of this book is to show you how you can best guard your estate so as to provide maximum income and security for your dependents. Here you will find a complete account of the estate and gift tax provisions, a discussion of methods of saving tax, and data to help you, plus 25 concrete and practical plans for preserving your hard-earned capital and assets. Readers of this book should also consult their attorney, accountant or trust adviser before making final decisions, so that the ideas offered here can be applied to particular circumstances in the best way.

Although How to Save Estate and Gift Taxes is written in clearly understandable non-technical terms, it will also be invaluable as a source of ideas for accountants, attorneys, bank officers, insurance men, and other advisers on estate problems. The 25 Tax-Saving Ideas particularly will help these specialists to offer imaginative and practical help to their clients.

This edition is completely up-to-date with all changes made by the most recent 1958 tax law.

Contents

Part One

25 TAX-SAVING IDEAS

1

Set Up a Grandfather's Insurance Trust

▶ *Man creates irrevocable living trust with cash or securities. Trust agreement directs trustee to take out insurance on son's life and use income from securities to pay premiums. The trust is beneficiary of the insurance. Grantor's grandchildren are remaindermen of trust.*

THE PROBLEM

Mr. Planner is 60 years of age. He has a substantial income —from a company that he owns, and from investments— and he pays a high rate of income tax.

His son, age 35, also has a big income. He is active in his father's business, will be president of it in a few years. No doubt he will have large salaries and dividends the rest of his life.

Mr. Planner, the father, wants to set aside some of his income-producing investments—some of the stock of his company, perhaps—in such a way that the income from these investments will be taxed at a low rate. As things stand, taxes are taking most of his dividends. It really will not cost him much to forego some of these dividends.

Give some stock to his son? He has already done that, and it would not help much to make further gifts, for the son too is in a high tax bracket.

3

Create typical irrevocable living trusts for the son's small children, Mr. Planner's grandchildren? That would offer advantages while the grandchildren are minors. But, under the law of Mr. Planner's State, income cannot be accumulated in trust for adults; so the accumulated income would have to go to the children when they became of age, and from then on they would have to receive the income as it was collected in the trust. The prospect of 21-year-olds having such large amounts of money did not fit in with Mr. Planner's ideas.

SOLUTION

Mr. Planner creates an irrevocable living trust for his grandchildren that, in effect, accumulates the income but does not violate the State law regarding accumulations.

He does so by providing that the trustee shall take out life insurance on his son's life and use the trust income to pay the premiums.

Specifically, Mr. Planner deposits $100,000 of his securities in the trust. These are producing about $5,000 income a year. In the trust agreement, Mr. Planner instructs the trustee to take out $100,000 insurance (whole-life policies, with the trust itself the beneficiary) on his son's life, using the income from the securities to pay the premiums. The premiums will be between $3,000 and $3,500 a year. Any income not used for premiums is to be paid Mr. Planner's son.

The trust is to last during the life of Mr. Planner's son. When the son dies, the trust will collect the $100,000 insurance proceeds and then will distribute among the son's children the entire trust principal—which, of course, will be $200,000 altogether if the securities are then worth $100,000.

Thus Mr. Planner's $100,000 grows to $200,000. If he had not created the trust, the $100,000—instead of doubling—might well have been cut in half by successive blows of the estate tax at his and his son's deaths.

TAXES

Under the trust plan, the $100,000 that Mr. Planner places in the trust will not be included in his estate for purposes of the Federal estate tax if he lives at least three years after creating the trust. The then value of the insurance policies would likewise not be taxed in his estate.

At the son's death, neither the securities nor the insurance proceeds will be included in the son's estate for Federal estate tax purposes. As to the insurance, remember that he does not own it.

Mr. Planner does have to pay a Federal gift tax upon creating the trust. The gift is $100,000, all of it a future interest. The gift tax would be $9,225 if Mr. Planner is a widower, only $2,400 if he is married and splits the gift with his wife (assuming they have not used any of their $30,000 lifetime exemptions up to this point).

As for the Federal income tax, the trust income used to pay the insurance premiums is taxed neither to Mr. Planner nor to his son; it is taxed to the trust itself. The trust's tax will not be a great deal, for its income in excess of its annual exemption will be taxed at the very lowest rates. The trust income distributable to the son will be taxed to him.

COMMENT 1. A "grandfather's insurance trust" like this may be particularly useful in a State like New York—which,

in general, does not permit accumulations for adult beneficiaries of trusts but which expressly permits the use of trust
income to pay insurance premiums. When income is used for
paying the premiums the effect is much as though the income
were being accumulated.

In other States that bar the accumulation of income for
adult beneficiaries, a trust of this nature may or may not
be valid. Legal advice should be obtained on the question.

In the States which do not prohibit the accumulation of
income for adults, the effects of a "grandfather's insurance
trust" might be largely obtained simply by having the trustee invest the income in stocks and bonds, rather than in
insurance, during the life of the grantor's son or daughter.
In that case, however, the amount of property eventually
going to the grandchildren can only be guessed at in ad-
vance; the son or daughter whose life measures the duration
of the trust may live for many years or, on the other hand,
but a short time. There may be advantages in the use of
insurance, therefore, even in New Jersey, Connecticut, and
other States that permit accumulations for adults; the insurance serves as a safeguard against the early death of the
grandchildren's parent, while at the same time serving as
an investment of the trust.

COMMENT 2. Where a "grandfather's insurance trust" is
used in a State that permits accumulations for adults, there
is no reason why the excess income—the amount not needed
for premiums—should not be accumulated. The trust agreement could provide that it be invested in stocks and bonds.
Thus, this excess income, as well as the amount needed for
premiums, could escape the high tax rates.

COMMENT 3. A "grandfather's insurance trust" would be distinctly less attractive if there should be any chance that the insurance proceeds would be taxed as a part of the insured person's estate—the estate of Mr. Planner's son, in our example.

It may be quite clear that the insured holds no incidents of ownership in the policies. But could it be claimed by the Government that the insured indirectly paid the premiums?

Possibly, in some situations, the son could be regarded as paying the premiums indirectly—especially if the trustee had some discretion, under the terms of the trust agreement, as to the amount of trust income going into insurance. But, since the 1954 tax law was enacted, this wouldn't matter. The 1954 law removed the "premium payment test," so that now the proceeds of a policy on a person's life are not ordinarily included in his estate for estate tax purposes unless he holds at his death an incident of ownership in the policy or its proceeds.

2

How to Make Sure an Estate Trust
Qualifies for the Marital Deduction

► *Husband's will leaves property in trust for widow. Income is payable to her for life and principal is payable to her estate. This trust can hold non-productive property or can accumulate income and still qualify for the estate tax marital deduction.*

THE PROBLEM

Mr. Planner owns all the stock of a small company. It is valuable stock but it has never paid a dividend. Mr. Planner would like to leave this stock in trust for his wife, with income going to her for life and with principal passing at her death to persons she names in her will to receive it. He wants the trust to qualify for the estate tax marital deduction.

But he is told there is some doubt that the trust would qualify for the deduction. *Reason:* The stock might be considered non-productive property, since it has never paid a dividend; and the estate tax Regulations on the marital deduction say that a power-of-appointment type of trust for the wife cannot qualify if it is substantially made up of non-productive property.

Perhaps if his company pays just one dividend during his

lifetime, or if it pays a dividend while the estate is being administered, the stock would not be regarded as non-productive property. But Mr. Planner's company is restricted in paying dividends—by an agreement with a lender, say —so a dividend could hardly be paid, not during the next few years anyway.

Of course, Mr. Planner could get a marital deduction if he should leave the stock to his wife outright. In the case of outright bequests, the property can be clearly non-productive and still it can qualify for the marital deduction. But Mr. Planner wants to leave it in trust. What can he do?

SOLUTION

Mr. Planner, in his will, leaves the stock (along with a little income-producing property, so that there will be enough cash for trustee's commissions) in trust for his wife. She is to receive the income, if there ever is any, while she lives. At her death the trust will end and the property in it will go to her estate.

This is not a trust in which there is a power of appointment involved in any way. Therefore the sections of the estate tax Regulations dealing with power-of-appointment trusts are inapplicable. It is only in these sections that a requirement is found that the property be productive.

But, if there is no power of appointment given the wife, can the trust qualify for the marital deduction? Yes, it can. Notice that the trust under Mr. Planner's will gives beneficial interests in property to no one but his wife. She is the only person interested in the property. Therefore, under the wording of the very first paragraph of section 2056 of the Internal Revenue Code—2056(a)—the trust would qualify.

It is not ruled out by the next-following paragraph—2056(b) —dealing with certain terminable interests.

COMMENT 1. A trust such as that established by Mr. Planner's will might also provide for an accumulation of income, as long as the accumulated income can go only to the wife or her estate. It is only in relation to power-of-appointment trusts that the law and Regulations require that the wife receive the income at least annually.

There may be an income tax saving from an accumulation.

EXAMPLE: *A man (living in a State where income of a trust can be accumulated for an adult) makes a will under which about half his estate is left in trust for his wife. Half the income of this trust is to be accumulated, half paid to her. When she dies the principal and the accumulation of income are to be paid her estate. After the husband dies, the widow will receive and be taxed for only half the income of the trust. The other half of the income will be taxed to the trust itself. Thus the income is divided between two taxpayers, and the total tax on it may be less than if the entire amount of income were taxed to the widow.*

This tax-saving trust would qualify for the estate tax marital deduction. No one but the widow has any beneficial interest in it whatever.

COMMENT 2. Another possible advantage of an "estate trust"—where the wife has no power to appoint the property but, instead, the property is definitely payable to her estate—

is that the wife may be able to leave the property in trust after her death for a longer period. Suppose, for example, she wants the property held in trust for her daughter's life, then for her granddaughter's life. She could set up such a trust in her will, under the laws of most States. She could, that is, if the property is made payable by her husband's will into her estate.

But if the husband's will gives her merely a power of appointment over the property, an attempt on her part to continue the property in trust would result, under the laws of most States, in a continuation of the trust under her husband's will. That is, the continuing trust would not be considered created by her, but by her husband. If she directs that the trust continue for two more lives—those of her daughter and her granddaughter—the total of three lives would be too long, under the laws of some States. And, if the granddaughter had not yet been born when the husband died, there would be an additional reason why the continuation of the trust might be invalid.

3

Make a Gift, Though in
Contemplation of Death

> ▶ *Aged person puts most of his property in irrevocable trust for children and dies two months later. Trust clearly is in contemplation of death. Yet it saves taxes, for the gift tax paid is, for Federal estate tax purposes, both a deduction from the gross estate and also a credit against the tax.*

Mrs. X, a widow aged 90, had $1,000,000. She put $700,000 of this into an irrevocable living trust for a grandson, her sole descendant. Two months later she died.

The trust represented a gift, of course, and Mrs. X's executor paid $153,000 Federal gift tax on account of it.

The gift was clearly "made in contemplation of death." So, for Federal estate tax purposes, the $700,000 in the trust was included in the estate. The total estate subject to the estate tax was . . .

Value of the property in the trust	$ 700,000
Mrs. X's other property	300,000
	$1,000,000
Less gift tax paid	153,000
Estate, before exemption	$ 847,000

The Federal estate tax on the $847,000 came to $222,000,

in round figures. From this the executor could deduct, as a credit, the $153,000 gift tax. The net Federal estate tax was, therefore, $69,000.

Altogether, the executor paid $153,000 gift tax and $69,000 estate tax, or a total of $222,000.

But if Mrs. X had not created the trust, and had died with an estate of $1,000,000, the Federal estate tax would have been just about $270,000.

The gift, though in contemplation of death, saved $48,000 tax!

COMMENT 1. Of course, more than $48,000 would have been saved if the gift had *not* been in contemplation of death—if Mrs. X, for example, had lived at least three years after making the gift; in which case the Government would not have been able to assert that contemplation of death was the motive.

The contemplation-of-death principle, in the case of Mrs. X, cut down the saving of tax. But it did not eliminate the saving entirely.

COMMENT 2. The example brings out the point that contemplation of death is not always a serious threat when an elderly person is considering large gifts to reduce the estate tax. In many cases it will be found that, even if the donor should die within three years and the contemplation-of-death motive cannot be disproved, there would be little if any tax disadvantage in making the gift. In effect, the payment of the gift tax is a pre-payment of the estate tax. The amount of gift tax paid is removed from the estate subject to the estate tax.

COMMENT 3. There will be a tax disadvantage from gifts in contemplation of death if the estate is not a large one like Mrs. X's. There would also be a disadvantage, probably, in any case where the credit for gift tax paid must be substantially reduced on account of a decline in the value of the gift property between the date of gift and the date of death.

But the larger the estate, and the greater the likelihood that the gift property will not decline in value, the greater is the probability that a gift will prove advantageous—and this is so regardless of the age and physical condition of the donor when the gift occurs.

COMMENT 4. In addition to considering the interplay of the estate tax and the gift tax when large gifts are planned, a study should be made also of the income tax effect of the proposed gift.

EXAMPLE: *Suppose the Mrs. X in our illustration deposited in the trust, as a part of the $700,000 total, a number of stocks in which she had large paper profits.*

After her death, and after the $700,000 has been included in her estate for estate tax purposes, what is the cost basis for income tax of these securities in the trust? The trustee gets a stepped-up basis equal to the value existing at Mrs. X's death. (This was a new provision in the 1954 tax law.)

But what if Mrs. X lives at least three years after creating the trust, so that the trust is *not* included in her estate under the contemplation-of-death rule or for any other reason?

In that case the trustee would have to use, as income tax costs, the low prices that were paid for the securities by Mrs. X. Considering both the estate tax advantage from the trust and the income tax disadvantage, it might have been better if Mrs. X had not created the trust after all. (To be considered here is a provision of the 1958 law. Under this provision, in certain circumstances, any Federal *gift* tax paid when a gift is made, either outright or in trust, increases the cost-basis of the property, for income tax purposes, in the hands of the donee or trustee. This means the seller will have a higher cost and smaller taxable profit.)

Therefore, if the donor has nothing but securities showing large profits, it may be inadvisable for him to create a trust such as Mrs. X's. It may be better for him to keep everything until he dies, so that the profits would surely escape income tax. If the donor has some securities showing profits and others which have costs approximating current market values, it would usually be advisable to select from the latter group in creating the trust.

COMMENT 5. Almost the same considerations—involving the estate tax, gift tax, and income tax—would apply to outright gifts as to gifts in trust like Mrs. X's. One possible difference: In the case of an outright gift made in contemplation of death, it appears that the amount to be included in the estate for Federal estate tax purposes is the value, at death, of the property given away—even though the donee may have sold those particular assets and re-invested in something else. In the case of a gift by means of an irrevocable trust, the property to be valued and included in the estate of the donor for estate tax purposes is whatever comprises the principal of the trust at death.

4

Assign Your Life Insurance

> *Husband assigns his insurance to his beneficiary or to a trustee but keeps on paying the premiums. Ordinarily, the proceeds will not be taxed in his estate.*

Most husbands own the insurance policies they have taken out for the protection of their wives and dependents—they own them in the sense that they can change the beneficiaries, borrow on the policies, assign them, etc.

Nine times out of ten these policies are payable direct to a named beneficiary, rather than to the husband's estate.

If a husband still owns policies like this at the time he dies, the full insurance proceeds are included in his estate for Federal estate tax purposes.

But if the husband does not own the policies when he dies—if, for example, he gave them to his wife some time before, making a complete and valid assignment of the contracts to her—then the proceeds are not ordinarily includible in his estate for tax purposes. This is so even though the husband continues to pay the premiums on the policies.

It was the 1954 tax law which brought about this situation. Formerly, insurance payable to a named beneficiary was included in the insured's estate for tax purposes if he owned the policy *or if he had paid the premiums*. The 1954 law removed the premium-payment test.

In the Senate, when this provision was being debated, it was said:

> It will be a simple matter indeed for an individual to plan his estate so as to exempt his life insurance from estate taxes. All he will have to do is make the policy payable to a designated beneficiary, without retaining the right to change the beneficiary and without retaining any other incidents of ownership in the policy.

There is no doubt that the new provision is decidedly favorable to taxpayers. The saving of tax, however, will not always be such a "simple matter." These considerations should be kept in mind:

1. If the insured person assigns his policies to his beneficiaries, then what happens if the beneficiary dies first? It would appear that the value of the policies would be included, for tax purposes, in the beneficiary's estate. Thus, a wholly unnecessary tax might be incurred.

2. The new law specifies that a "reversionary interest" retained by the insured shall—if it is worth more than 5% of the value of the policy—be considered a form of ownership. It matters not, says the law, whether such an interest is set forth expressly in the policy or arises by operation of law. Thus, the insured would be right back where he started if, after giving away a policy, he had better than one chance in 20 to regain the value of the policy at some time in the future.

3. After all, if an insured person gives his policies to his beneficiary, he is parting with control over the property. Will the beneficiary keep the policies for the protective purposes for which they were intended? If there are any doubts

in this respect, an irrevocable assignment of the contracts might be most unwise.

4. A gift of insurance policies may call for the payment of a Federal gift tax. The same could be true of the payment of premiums on the policies after they have been given away. Thus, the probable saving of estate tax may not represent the real, net saving; the gift tax may partially offset it.

5. It may be that, if a large insurance policy should be given away by the insured within three years of his death, the proceeds would be included in his estate for tax purposes under the "contemplation-of-death" rule. Thus, the tax saving from the gift might be far less than expected.

▶ There is no need to worry about the "transfers-taking-effect-at-death" provision in the tax law, however. That provision is of narrower application than the provision dealing specifically with life insurance. In other words, if insurance is not included in the insured person's taxable estate under the provision dealing with insurance, it could not possibly be included in the estate under the "transfers-taking-effect-at-death" rule.

Perhaps some of the above considerations could be eliminated if the insured person assigns his policies—not to his dependent-beneficiary—but to an irrevocable insurance trust.

EXAMPLE: *John Planner—who carries a considerable amount of insurance with his wife named as beneficiary— assigns his policies to a trustee. In an irrevocable trust agreement, he instructs the trustee to collect*

> *the proceeds at his death, to invest them, and to*
> *pay the income to his widow. If extra funds*
> *should be needed in emergencies, the trustee is*
> *to pay some of the principal, in addition to the*
> *income, to the widow. At her death the trust is to*
> *end and the property is to be divided among the*
> *children.*
>
> *Mr. Planner continues to pay the premiums on the*
> *policies.*

An insurance trust of this nature offers advantages wholly apart from taxes. It frees the widow from the responsibility of investing the funds upon which she and the children are dependent. It tends to "make the money last longer." The eventual distribution of the principal to the children is assured.

From a tax standpoint, such a trust could definitely remove the possibility that the value of the insurance would be taxed in the beneficiary's estate, whether the beneficiary dies before or after the insured. Moreover, the trust agreement could be so drawn that no reversionary interest in the policies would be kept by the person whose life is insured.

But against these advantages, there is to be considered a possible disadvantage in connection with the Federal gift tax—namely, that the gifts would be considered "future interests," with a consequent loss of the $3,000 annual exclusion.

Why should a husband go to the trouble of assigning his insurance to his wife or to a trustee if, as is usually the case, the policies would qualify for the estate tax marital deduction when he dies? This point becomes somewhat complicated at times, but estate tax computations will show that it pays to eliminate assets from the taxable estate even though those very assets would, if left in the estate, give rise to a marital deduction. Other assets can be utilized for the marital deduction. The deduction is always limited to roughly half the taxable estate. The elimination from the estate of property passing to the wife reduces the maximum marital deduction but it also reduces the half of the estate that is left to be taxed after the marital deduction is taken off.

5
Make a Will

► *Without a will, the widow may get only one-third the estate—less than the maximum marital deduction. Also, only by making a will can you leave property in trust to avoid estate tax at your beneficiary's death.*

Mr. A lives in a State where, if a husband leaves no will, the widow gets one-third of his property and the children get two-thirds. Mr. A owns property worth $200,000. All of this property will pass through the hands of his executor. He has no life insurance payable direct to a named beneficiary, and he has no jointly owned property. He estimates that his administrative estate and also his estate for tax purposes will be $200,000.

If he leaves no will, therefore, his widow will receive $66,666. That will be the marital deduction. The Federal estate tax on the estate will be $12,966.

(For simplicity, it is assumed that the adjusted gross estate—after debts and expenses are paid—is $200,000. It is assumed also that no State or Federal tax will be taken out of the widow's intestate share; which, as to the Federal tax at least, appears to be the rule in most States.)

Mr. A can save more than $8,000 Federal estate tax simply by making a will and leaving *half* his estate to his wife. If he leaves her $100,000, the marital deduction will be

$100,000. The Federal estate tax will be only $4,800 . . . lower by $8,166 than the $12,966 tax that is payable if he leaves no will.

Mr. B's case is even more startling. He has $200,000 of property that will pass through the hands of his executor, and he also carries $50,000 life insurance. The insurance is payable for his wife's benefit under one of the options—the option in this case being one which does not qualify for the marital deduction.

In Mr. B's State also the widow gets only a third of the estate if the husband leaves no will. But note this: the share going to the widow is one-third of the administrative estate only. In other words, if Mr. B leaves no will, Mrs. B will receive a third of $200,000, or $66,666, and not one-third of the tax estate of $250,00.

So, if Mr. B leaves no will, the marital deduction will be $66,666. The Federal estate tax will be $26,766.

By leaving a will and giving Mrs. B half of his taxable estate, or $125,000, Mr. B can reduce the Federal estate tax to $10,700. The will can save approximately $16,000 in tax!

How much would Mr. A and Mr. B pay their lawyers to have their wills drawn? Any reasonable fee would be insignificant compared to the $8,166 that a will would save for Mr. A's family . . . or the $16,000 that could be saved for Mr. B's family.

Apart from taxes, there are any number of advantages in having a will. Here are just two:

1. In a will you can select the person or organization you wish to settle your estate . . . instead of having the court appoint someone—someone, perhaps, whom you would never have chosen for the work.

2. In a will you can leave your property in trust for your beneficiaries . . . instead of having it all go in a lump sum to beneficiaries who may not be prepared to manage the property, and who might quickly lose or squander it.

Advantage No. 2, mentioned immediately above, brings up another possible tax saving in having a will: you can, by means of a will, leave your property in trust for your beneficiary so as to eliminate an estate tax on the property when the beneficiary dies.

If you do not leave a will, your property goes outright to your beneficiaries (in most States). When your beneficiaries die, there may be an estate tax on the property even though that very same property had been taxed in your estate not so many years earlier.

Here is an example of a trust set up in a will:

Mrs. Planner is a widow. She owns property valued at $200,000. If she leaves this outright to her daughter, there will be a Federal estate tax at Mrs. Planner's death in amount of $31,500. Then, if the daughter should die more than ten years later, and leave the property inherited from her mother ($200,000 less $31,500) to her children, there would be a Federal estate tax of approximately $22,500. The two taxes—at Mrs. Planner's death and at the daughter's death—would total $54,000.

Mrs. Planner can eliminate entirely the $22,500 tax at her daughter's death by leaving her $200,000 estate in trust for the daughter. Under the terms of Mrs. Planner's will, the daughter would receive the income for life (and some of the principal too if, in the trustee's opinion, she needed extra money in emergencies). Then, at the daughter's death, Mrs. Planner's will provides that the trustee shall distribute the principal of the trust among the daughter's children then living. (Or Mrs. Planner's will could give the daughter a limited power of appointment over the trust principal.)

Mrs. Planner, by making a will and setting up a simple trust for her daughter, saves $22,500 tax.

The saving from making a will and leaving property in trust may be even greater if the trust lasts during two successive lives. For example, suppose Mrs. Planner had provided that, at her daughter's death, the trust should continue for benefit of the daughter's daughter—Mrs. Planner's granddaughter. In that case the Federal estate tax on the money left by Mrs. Planner could be eliminated not only at the daughter's death, but also at the granddaughter's death. *Two* estates are "by-passed" by means of the trusts.

6

Consider an Insurance Trust to Raise Cash to Pay Estate Tax

► *The proceeds of the policies go to a trustee, who is empowered in the trust agreement (which is revocable) to buy hard-to-sell assets from the estate or to loan money to the estate. Thus the estate gets needed cash, yet the insurance proceeds escape settlement costs and the State inheritance tax (in many States).*

If a person makes his insurance policies payable to his estate (to his executor, that is), there are these points to consider:

1. The proceeds will be taxable under the Federal estate tax.
2. The proceeds will be taxable under the State inheritance tax.
3. Executor's commissions will be taken on the proceeds.
4. The insurance proceeds will be subject to claims against the estate.

"But I must make my insurance—some of it, at least—payable to my executor," a man says. "My executor is going to need cash to pay taxes, expenses, etc."

You can make cash from your insurance available to your

executor and still eliminate the possible disadvantages represented by points 2, 3, and 4, above.

EXAMPLE: *Jones carries $100,000 life insurance. He names as beneficiary of this insurance the XYZ Bank & Trust Company, as trustee. In an insurance trust agreement (drawn by his lawyer), he instructs the trustee to collect the $100,000 when he dies and to invest the money, paying the income to his wife as long as she lives.*

So far, we have an ordinary insurance trust. How can the cash proceeds of the insurance be made available to the executor?

There is a paragraph in the insurance trust agreement that does the trick. It authorizes the trustee to buy, at a fair price, assets of the estate from the executor. It also authorizes the trustee to lend money to the executor, with or without collateral.

The executor of the estate may be the same XYZ Bank & Trust Company that is trustee under the insurance trust, so the two parties—the executor and the trustee—should not have much difficulty in coming to an agreement as to price. Also, the residuary legatee under the will is likely to be the widow; and if she is also the income beneficiary of the insurance trust, and if she is to have some of the principal too of the insurance trust under certain conditions, there cannot be much conflict of interests between the estate and the trust.

Does this arrangement save Federal estate tax? No, for if the insured holds any incident of ownership in the policies when he dies, the proceeds will be included in his estate for purposes of the Federal estate tax. This trust, we have assumed, is revocable; the insured always has the right to change his plans to meet new developments. He cannot, under these conditions, hope to have the insurance excluded from his estate for Federal tax purposes.

Does this arrangement always save State inheritance or state tax? Not in all States, for some States follow the Federal rule as to taxation of insurance proceeds, or have an estate tax which, in amount, is the allowable credit under the Federal tax, no more and no less. But in many States insurance *is* taxed if it is payable to the estate and *is not* taxed if it is payable to a named beneficiary. The trustee of the insurance trust qualifies as a named beneficiary. It is in this latter group of States that the insurance trust saves the State tax.

Even where the State tax is saved, is there an over-all saving? Is not the saving of State tax cancelled out by the fact that the State tax can be used as a credit against the Federal tax? In many States there is an over-all saving. The State tax, for example, may exceed the amount that the Federal tax law permits as a credit. In these circumstances a reduction of the State tax, up to a certain point, has no effect on the amount of the allowable credit, and a clear saving results.

Is not the saving of executor's commissions offset by the trustee's commissions that must be paid? The saving here depends on whether the insured person wants his property distributed outright or left in trust. If he favors a trust arrangement—and often this is the only practical course if the wife or other beneficiary is unskilled in handling investments—there is usually a considerable saving of commissions in having the insurance proceeds paid into an insurance trust rather than having them paid to the executor.

If paid to the executor, there will of course be executor's commissions. Then, if the will leaves the estate, including the insurance, in a trust for the wife or children, there will be the commissions of the trustee. The practice here varies, but in some States it is entirely proper for the executor and trustee to take so-called "double commissions"—once as executor and once as trustee—on the very same property. There is nothing wrong about such a practice, for if an amount first passes through the estate and then is set up in a trust, the services of the executor-trustee are just about doubled and the two commissions are earned.

Now, if the insured leaves his insurance money in an insurance trust, there is only one commission—that of the trustee under the insurance trust. The executor of the estate ordinarily gets no commission on these insurance proceeds even though he sells assets to the trust or borrows money from it.

Then the insured may have two trusts for his beneficiaries —one under the insurance trust agreement and one under the will? He may, if he wishes to leave the residue of his estate in trust for his beneficiaries. This may not be the ideal plan in all cases, especially if each trust is a small one. Investing the money of two small trusts is more of a problem than investing for one larger fund. Moreover, the trustee's commissions (which are usually graduated *downward* as the size of the fund increases) may be larger. But two separate funds do offer the possibility of saving income taxes, in certain circumstances. Each trust will be taxed for its own capital gains; and, if the income is accumulated, each trust pays a tax on its own interest and dividends. Two separate trusts might well pay less income tax than one larger trust reporting the total income.

If, however, the possibility of saving income tax on accumulated income and capital gains is not an important factor, the insured person may be able to simplify his plans by providing that one fund shall be "poured over" into the other. He could, for example, provide in his will that the residue of his estate shall be paid by his executor to the trustee of the insurance trust, to be held and managed by the trustee along with the insurance proceeds.

"Pour overs" like this, from the estate to the insurance trust, appear to be sound planning in most States. The advice of a lawyer, of course, is needed on this point in every instance. "Pour overs" in the opposite direction, however—from the insurance fund to a trust created by the will —may be impractical or impossible.

7

Be Careful of a Common-Disaster Clause in a Married Person's Will

▶ *A common-disaster clause in a husband's will may cancel a bequest to his wife, and thus destroy a marital deduction. Since 1948 it is often better to have no common-disaster clause in the husband's will. It may even be advisable to have a "reverse" clause, making sure that the bequest goes through the wife's estate.*

Suppose a husband, in his will, gives his wife $100,000 and then provides, in effect . . .

"But if she does not survive me by 30 days, then this $100,000 shall not go to her or her estate, but shall go to my son."

If it were not for the Federal estate tax, such a clause as this probably would always be good planning on the husband's part. If his wife is living after 30 days, then she receives the bequest. But if she is not—if, for example, she and her husband are in an automobile accident, and she dies an hour or two after he dies—what would be the sense in having the husband's executor pay the money to the wife's executor, who then would pay it to the son? It would be more economical and quicker to have the money go direct to the son.

But, with the Federal estate tax taken into consideration, it may be considerably more economical to have the $100,000 take the round-about course, passing through the wife's estate though she survives but a short time. Here is why:

If the bequest goes through the wife's estate, the husband's estate gets a marital deduction for the amount of the bequest. If, under the terms of a common-disaster clause, the bequest by-passes the wife's estate and goes direct to the son, the husband's estate does not get a marital deduction.

The tax saved in the husband's estate by the marital deduction may exceed the expense in having the money pass through the wife's estate.

EXAMPLE: *Altogether, the husband's estate is $200,000. If $100,000 is left to the wife, the Federal estate tax on his estate (thanks to the marital deduction) is only $4,800. If there is no bequest to the wife to qualify for the marital deduction, the Federal estate tax on his estate will be $31,500.*

Having the $100,000 pass to the wife or her estate, therefore, reduces the Federal tax on the husband's estate by $26,700.

Now, how much would it *cost* to have the $100,000 pass through the wife's estate? In Federal estate tax it would cost only $4,800, if she had no other property to be taxed. In addition, there would possibly be a State inheritance tax and certain expenses connected with settling her estate— executor's commissions and attorney's fees, for example. Let's say these items total $5,000. In all, therefore, the cost of having the bequest go through the wife's estate would be $10,000, approximately.

Comparing the $10,000 cost with the $26,700 tax saved in

the husband's estate, a substantial net saving is apparent.

It is this net saving that may be jeopardized by a common-disaster clause in the husband's will. It might pay him, if he now has a will containing such a clause, to have a new will drawn, giving his wife a share of his estate provided only that she survive him.

Perhaps the husband's will should even go further than that. Perhaps his will should provide that his wife shall receive the bequest if she survive him *or if he and she die in a common disaster and it cannot be determined which survived the other*. If he does not make this provision regarding their deaths in a common disaster, the law of his State probably would require the presumption that she died first, and therefore she would not inherit from him. He can overcome this presumption (it is in the law of nearly all the States) by clearly instructing in his will that the bequest shall pass through his wife's estate if the order of deaths cannot be determined.

The point we have been discussing—the inadvisability of the usual type of common-disaster provision in a husband's will—should not be given undue emphasis. It is hardly necessary for a husband, if he finds a bequest to his wife coupled with a common-disaster provision, to rush out and have his will changed immediately.

It is only if there should be a common disaster, or successive deaths within 30 days or other stipulated period, that the common-disaster provision in a will has any effect whatever. If the wife is known to die before the husband, or if she survives the stipulated period, the provision in the will does no harm. The Federal estate tax law makes it clear that a bequest to the wife conditioned on her surviving for a period up to six months qualifies for the marital deduction if she does in fact survive.

EXAMPLE: *Husband leaves $10,000 to wife provided she is living six months after date of his death. She does survive him by six months and receives the $10,000. Result: Husband's estate is entitled to a marital deduction for the $10,000 bequest, even though when he died it could not be known that she would receive the bequest.*

It would be advisable, however, to make certain that a common-disaster clause in the husband's will falls within the type permitted by the Federal estate tax. For example, if a husband leaves a house to his wife "provided she shall live in it for a period of at least six months after my death," the gift would not qualify for the marital deduction even if the wife should stay in the house for six months and take title to it. The condition attached to the gift by the husband is not within the class that is "overlooked," you might say, by the estate tax, for it requires that she not only live for six months but also that she retain her residence for that period.

Here is the exact wording of the law dealing with common-disaster clauses:

Where, on the lapse of time, on the occurrence of an event or contingency, or on the failure of an event or contingency to occur, an interest passing to the surviving spouse will terminate or fail, no deduction shall be allowed with respect to such interest—

(A) if an interest in such property passes or has passed (for less than an adequate and full consideration in money or money's worth) from the decedent to any person other than such surviving spouse (or the estate of such spouse); and

(B) if by reason of such passing such person (or his heirs or assigns) may possess or enjoy any part of such property after such termination or failure of the interest so passing to the surviving spouse. (*IRC. sec. 2056(b) (1)*)

For the purposes of this subsection, an interest passing to the surviving spouse shall not be considered as an interest which will terminate or fail upon the death of such spouse if—

(A) such death will cause a termination or failure of such interest only if it occurs within a period not exceeding six months after the decedent's death, or only if it occurs as a result of a common disaster resulting in the death of the decedent and the surviving spouse, or only if it occurs in the case of either such event; and

(B) such termination or failure does not in fact occur. (*IRC. sec. 2056(b)(3)*)

Get a Gift Tax Exclusion for Gifts to Trusts for Minors

▶ *Parent or grandparent creates irrevocable living trust for minor children. Gift tax results under the 1954 tax law.*

Parents of small children sometimes approach banks and trust companies with plans like this:

"I'd like to put aside a few thousand dollars each year for my son. You are to invest the money and accumulate the income until he is 21. Then he is to have the entire fund—principal and income."

Such an arrangement fits in nicely with the financial plans of many families—and it also may result in a reduction of income taxes. If the money is put in an irrevocable living trust, the income from the investments would be taxed to the trust itself and not to the parent who creates the trust. The trust, in most cases, would pay a far lower rate of tax on it than the parent would.

In the past, however, there has been a disadvantage connected with the trust arrangement: the amounts deposited each year by the parent have been considered gifts of "future interests." Consequently the $3,000 annual exemption, or "exclusion," from the Federal gift tax has not been allowed.

(Actually, this exemption works out to $6,000 a year if the parents "split" the gifts.) The trust idea has therefore compared unfavorably with other financial arrangements that might be made for the child's benefit.

► The 1954 tax law provides that, after 1954, gifts to a minor shall not be considered gifts of future interests if the income and property can be spent by or for the child and, to the extent not so spent, will pass to the child when he becomes 21 (or to his estate or as he may "appoint," under certain conditions, if he dies before 21).

The effect of this new provision should be discussed with your lawyer. It may be possible, however, that an accumulation trust for a child can now be so drawn that contributions to it would qualify for the gift-tax annual exemptions. The trustee, no doubt, would have to be authorized to make emergency payments, at least, from the principal and accumulated income if the child should ever be in need of funds. But such a provision in an accumulation trust is usually considered wise in any event, and should make the trust no less attractive from the parent's viewpoint.

But the parent, in a great many cases, may not consider it advisable to have all the principal and income paid to the child as soon as he is 21. The new provision, however, appears to require this, if the gift tax exclusions are to be had and if the income during minority is to be accumulated.

In considering the Federal gift tax as it applies to children's trusts, it should be noted that useful and tax-economi-

cal arrangements are possible without the benefit of the
new provision of the 1954 tax law.

As an example, suppose that a man wishes to put aside
money each year in a trust for his 10-year-old son. But he
wants the trust to continue after the son is 21—until he is
30, for example. The son, when he reaches 21, is to receive
the income that has been accumulated up to that point, and
between ages 21 and 30 the son is to have the income as it
is collected.

When the son becomes 30 the trust is to end. But the
property in it is to be paid—not to the son—but to the
father. The father desires to support the son until his education is completed and he has begun to support himself
comfortably. But the father feels that he cannot afford to
let the son have all the money then; he, the father, may
need it for his retirement.

Under such a trust the father may find that his gift tax
liability is little indeed. It is true that he gets no annual
exemptions as to the amounts he deposits in the trust while
the son is a minor. But only a portion of each such deposit
is a gift of any kind (because the father himself will someday get back the principal). And the portions which represent gifts may not add up to the lifetime exemptions of the
child's parents, so that no tax at all may be called for.

9

Give Trustee the Power to Pay Principal Instead of Giving Beneficiary the Right to Withdraw Principal

▶ *If the beneficiary of a trust is authorized by the will or trust agreement to withdraw principal, the principal may be includible in the beneficiary's estate for Federal estate tax purposes. In some situations there may be liability for Federal gift tax too. The beneficiary may also be taxed for capital gains in the trust. A safer plan is to empower the trustee, in its discretion, to pay principal to the beneficiary.*

THE PROBLEM

A trust—living or testamentary—will be more adaptable to changing conditions if some provision is made in the will or trust agreement for payments of principal, in addition to the income, to the beneficiary. Moreover, the income beneficiary is usually the chief object of concern of the person who creates the trust; the welfare of the trust remaindermen is a distant problem. Sometimes the remaindermen are not even known to the person making the trust, or are not yet born when the trust is created.

38

But if the beneficiary is permitted to withdraw principal at will and without any questions asked, the fund may be dissipated in short order. It may leave the beneficiary stranded.

And, from a tax standpoint, there are these further considerations:

Federal Estate Tax: A beneficiary who can withdraw all the principal of the trust at any time is considered to have a general power of appointment over the fund. Thus, if the trust was created after October 21, 1942, the principal will be included in the beneficiary's estate for Federal estate tax purposes.

Federal Income Tax: Capital gains in the trust are not ordinarily taxed to the beneficiary; instead, they are reported by the trust itself. But the beneficiary *is* taxed for such gains if he or she has the right to withdraw all the principal at any time.

"I'll limit my beneficiary's right to withdraw funds to a certain amount a year," a man says when he is creating a trust.

First, he must decide whether the right is to be cumulative or non-cumulative. A cumulative right would be one where, if the beneficiary fails to withdraw the stipulated sum this year, he can double up next year; and if he does not withdraw anything next year, he can carry forward the total to the year after that, and so on. In time, if the beneficiary does not withdraw any principal, he may have the right to withdraw the entire fund at one time, and the estate tax and income tax rules given above would apply to his situation.

More often the beneficiary's right is non-cumulative. If he has the right to withdraw, say, $10,000 a year, he cannot have more than that amount in any year though he may not have taken all he could have in prior years. If, in any year, he fails to withdraw all he is entitled to for that year, his right lapses.

Any such lapse is treated under the Federal estate and gift tax, it seems, as though the beneficiary had withdrawn the amount and then put it right back again in the trust. *Result, if the trust was created after October 21, 1942:* Federal gift tax liability (because, if a deposit is considered to have been made to the trust, a gift is made to the trust remaindermen), and also Federal estate tax liability (because the gift "takes effect" at the beneficiary's death).

Under both the estate and gift tax, however, a lapse is disregarded unless it exceeds (1) $5,000, or (2) an amount equal to 5% of the value of the fund, whichever is greater. Only the excess is taken into account.

EXAMPLE: *A widow is beneficiary of a trust under her deceased husband's will. He died after October 21, 1942. She can have up to $10,000 of principal paid to her each year. This right is non-cumulative.*

In 1958 she does not withdraw any principal. The trust property is valued at the end of 1958 at $150,000. 5% of this value is $7,500.

The $10,000 that the widow could have withdrawn but didn't is $2,500 in excess of this $7,500 exemption. For gift and estate tax purposes she is considered to have released a general power of appointment over the $2,500.

For gift tax, it would seem that the widow should be permitted to reduce the $2,500 by the value of her remaining life estate in $2,500, for she herself is the beneficiary of the trust. For estate tax, the Regulations call for an adjustment in the $2,500 to compensate for increase or decrease in the value of the trust property between the date of the lapse and the date of the widow's death; and presumably credit could be taken against the estate tax for any gift tax paid when the lapse occurred.

SOLUTIONS

The complexities of the tax situation, as described above, are enough to discourage anyone from giving a beneficiary the right to withdraw large sums of principal from a trust annually. What, then, can be done to protect the beneficiary in the event of a sudden and unexpected need for cash?

There are three possibilities:

1. The will or trust agreement can be so drawn that the beneficiary cannot have more than $5,000 of principal in any year, or more than 5% of the value of the fund, whichever is greater.

2. The beneficiary's right to withdraw principal could be limited, by the terms of the will or trust agreement, by an ascertainable standard relating to the beneficiary's education, health, support, or maintenance. (Under the powers-of-appointment provisions of the estate and gift tax laws, the beneficiary then would *not* have a general power of appointment.)

3. *The best plan, in nearly every situation, will be to leave payments from principal wholly to the trustee's discretion.* For example, the will or trust agreement could

authorize the trustee to pay some of the principal, in addition to income, to the beneficiary if the trustee at any time thought the beneficiary needed extra money for medical expenses or other purposes.

Under the third plan—where payments from principal are in the discretion of the trustee—the beneficiary is given the fullest protection possible. Yet the beneficiary, under this plan, has none of the estate and gift tax problems that would usually result from his or her own control over the fund. Neither would there be any possibility that the capital gains of the trust would be taxed to the beneficiary.

10

When to Use Limited Instead of General Power of Appointment

> ▶ *A limited power of appointment is often more advantageous. It will not cause the property to be taxed (Federal estate tax) in the beneficiary's estate. A power may be quite broad and still qualify as a limited power for Federal estate tax purposes.*

THE PROBLEM

Mr. Planner, when he had his will drawn, told his lawyer that he wanted to leave part of his estate in trust for his married daughter. "She is to have the income as long as she lives, and when she dies the property in the trust is to go to whomever she names to receive it in her will. She is to have absolutely a free hand in this respect."

The daughter, under such a will, would be said to have a "general" power of appointment over the trust fund. And the mere possession of such a power, the lawyer pointed out to Mr. Planner, would make the entire principal of the trust fund includible in the daughter's estate for Federal estate tax purposes.

"I can't help it," Mr. Planner said. "I am not in a position to decide who should have the property when my daughter dies. I can't see that far into the future."

43

SOLUTION

But the lawyer suggested a simple change in the proposed will—a change that would eliminate the Federal estate tax on the property at the daughter's death yet which would still give the daughter broad control over the disposition of the property. All Mr. Planner had to do, the lawyer said, was to provide in his will that his daughter should *not* have the right to have the property distributed to herself, her estate, or the creditors of herself or of her estate.

This would make her power of appointment "limited" rather than "general." The possession by the daughter of a limited power of appointment—or even the exercise of such a power—would not cause the property to be included in her estate for Federal estate tax purposes.

The daughter, under her limited power, would be able to apportion the property among her children in any way she wished. She could give some or all of the property to her husband. She could even have the property go to non-relatives. But, since she could not "appoint" the property to herself, her creditors, her estate, or the creditors of her estate, there would be no estate tax on it when she died.

COMMENT 1: By limiting the power a little more, Mr. Planner might also save a State inheritance tax at his daughter's death. In some States the possession or exercise of a general power is taxed, but limited powers are not; and the definition of a general power under the State law may therefore be worth considering. Of course, the person who leaves property in trust, such as Mr. Planner in our example, cannot know for sure in which State his daughter will be living when she dies.

COMMENT 2: If the beneficiary of the trust is the wife or husband of the one who creates the trust—if Mr. Planner, for example, had been considering a trust for his wife instead of his daughter—the type of power of appointment given the beneficiary would have an effect on the estate tax when the creator of the trust dies.

Suppose a husband leaves property in trust for his wife, giving her all the income for life and also giving her a general power of appointment over the principal when she dies. This trust would qualify for the marital deduction, thereby possibly reducing the Federal estate tax at the husband's death by thousands of dollars. But if the power of appointment given the wife should be limited, *the trust would not qualify for the marital deduction in the husband's estate.*

In view of this situation, the so-called "two-trust" arrangement often proves to be the most economical in the husband's will. If he creates two trusts for his wife, each for about half of his estate, he can give his wife a general power of appointment as to one of them and a limited power, or no power at all, as to the other. The net effect of such an arrangement often is that half his property is taxed when he dies (because the trust with the general power gives his estate a marital deduction) and half is taxed when his widow dies later (because the trust with the limited power is not included in her estate). The aggregate tax on the husband's property, when it is "split" in this way, may be much less than if all the property were taxed in one of the estates.

COMMENT 3: In connection with Comment (2), above, it should be noted that the estate tax definition of a power of appointment sufficient to qualify a trust for the marital deduction is not quite the same as the definition, in the estate tax and gift tax, of a general power of appointment. For marital deduction purposes, the power must enable the surviving spouse to appoint the property to herself or to her estate. Under the definition of a general power, on the other hand, the beneficiary must have the right to appoint the property to herself or her estate *or her creditors or the creditors of her estate.* The slight distinction appears to be significant only to the lawyer who drafts the will; it would be unfortunate indeed if, by a slip of the pen, the husband's will should create a power of appointment sufficient to make the property taxable in his wife's estate but insufficient to entitle his own estate to a marital deduction.

COMMENT 4: In the case of an irrevocable living trust created by a husband for his wife, the type of power of appointment—general or limited—would have a bearing on Federal gift tax liability.

If the wife-beneficiary is given a power to appoint the property to herself or her estate (whether or not she can appoint to others), the husband may be entitled to a gift tax marital deduction for half the value of the property he puts in the trust.

If, on the other hand, the wife-beneficiary cannot appoint to herself or her estate, there would be no marital deduction available. In these circumstances, however, the husband and wife could possibly "split" the gift represented by the remainder of the trust.

EXAMPLE: *Husband puts $100,000 in an irrevocable living trust for his wife, whose age is 60. She is to receive the income for life, but she has not the power to appoint the principal.*

Under the mortality table in the gift tax Regulations, about 60¢ of every dollar put in the trust would be considered a gift to the remaindermen of the trust. $60,000, therefore, is the value of this gift; and, under the split-gift provisions of the Federal gift tax, the husband and wife could agree that each would report half, or $30,000.

The husband would also have to report as a gift the value of the wife's life estate, less a $3,000 annual exclusion. He could not cut this gift in half with a gift tax marital deduction, for he has not given his wife a power of appointment over the trust.

11

Use Insurance on Wife's Life to Hedge against Taxes

► *Life insurance, taken out by husband on life of wife, can compensate for loss of the marital deduction if she dies first (Federal estate tax); also for loss of joint-return privilege (Federal income tax).*

FEDERAL ESTATE TAX

Mr. Planner owns property valued at $200,000. His wife has little or no property of her own. He has made a will under which (thanks to the marital deduction) half his property will be taxed when he dies and half will be taxed when she dies . . . and the Federal estate tax will be only $4,800 in each of the two estates, or less than $10,000 altogether.

This will be the tax result, that is, if he dies first. If she dies first, there will be no marital deduction for his estate, and the Federal estate tax will be $31,500!

Mr. Planner can protect his children against the $21,500 higher tax by taking out at least $21,500 insurance on his wife's life.

The children can be named beneficiaries. Mr. Planner pays the premiums but he assigns the policy to his wife. His premium payments would represent gifts to her, but they

48

would be gifts of present interests and therefore would be cancelled out by the $3,000 annual exclusion for gift tax.

If Mrs. Planner dies first, the proceeds going to the children (under an optional method of settlement, possibly) would compensate for the higher tax that will be paid from their father's estate eventually. The proceeds would be includible in Mrs. Planner's estate for Federal estate tax purposes, but of course her estate would pay no tax because it would be less than the $60,000 exemption.

If Mr. Planner dies first, it would appear unlikely that the then value of the policy could be included in his estate for Federal estate tax purposes. Mrs. Planner, afterwards, could either surrender the policy for cash or give it to the children; if she retained it, her estate tax liabilities would be increased.

FEDERAL INCOME TAX

Mr. Planner's income, after exemptions and deductions, is $32,000 . . . Mrs. Planner has no income of her own. On a joint Federal income tax return they can "split" the $32,000 and pay a tax of $10,400. But if Mrs. Planner should be the first to die, Mr. Planner would have to pay a tax of $14,460.

(Taxes are figured at the 1958 rates. It is assumed that Mr. Planner, if a widower, would not qualify as "head of a household," nor would he be entitled to "split" his income for any period after his wife's death.)

In view of the $4,000-a-year higher income tax that would be payable if Mrs. Planner should die first, her husband might reasonably take out insurance on her life in an amount of, say, five times the annual "loss," or $20,000.

This insurance, like that to protect against loss of the estate tax marital deduction, could be assigned to the wife and made payable to the children. The children are the ultimate "losers," if either of their parents pay unexpectedly high taxes; therefore the policies may as well be payable to them, reducing the tax liabilities on the insurance itself.

In the case of Mr. and Mrs. Planner, this would mean that they would need to take out somewhat over $40,000 in all . . . about half of which would be for protection against higher estate tax if the wife dies first, and the other half protecting against the higher income tax that would result from loss of the "split-income" privilege.

12

Benefit from a Short-Term Trust for Your Parents

> ► *An irrevocable living trust for benefit of an aged parent or other relative, with principal coming back to the grantor at the beneficiary's death, can save income tax. Yet it costs little or nothing in gift tax, for the only gift is the life estate in the property put in the trust.*

THE PROBLEM

Mr. Planner has been sending his mother $200 a month. She desperately needs the money for living expenses. But there are two things wrong with the arrangement:

1. The mother is unhappy in being always dependent on her son for her support; and

2. Mr. Planner cannot take income tax deductions for the amounts he gives her.

Mr. Planner cannot even claim his mother as his dependent for income tax purposes, for she does have a little income of her own (more than $600, that is). He is paying income tax at a top rate of about 50%. The $2,400 a year that he sends her really has been taking about $5,000 of his income, with taxes considered.

SOLUTION

Finally he does find a way to get tax deductions, in a sense, for the payments to his mother:

He puts about $50,000 of his securities in an irrevocable living trust for benefit of his mother. The income, which will amount to about $2,400 a year after the trustee has taken its commission, is payable to the mother as long as she lives. When she dies the trust is to end and the principal is to come back to Mr. Planner or, if he is not then living, to his estate.

From then on, Mr. Planner is not taxed for the income from these securities. His mother is taxed for the amounts distributable to her. But, since she has little other income, and has a doubled exemption for being over 65, and can deduct every dollar of her medical expenses up to the maximum, she pays very little income tax.

And the tax that she does pay is not without its compensations to her, for it contributes to her new-found sense of independence. No longer is she constantly receiving from her son the payments that were tinged with the characteristics of handouts. Instead, she has her own trust fund at the bank, and her checks that come to her regularly in the mail are hers by right.

This trust arrangement, that seems so ideally suited to the situation and which saves Mr. Planner about $1,200 in taxes every year . . . are there no "catches" to it? No, there are not. Consider these points:

Income Tax: The mother, at the time the trust is created, is well up in her seventies. Her life expectancy according to the mortality tables is less than ten years. Now, there are income tax rules—see section 673 of the Internal Revenue Code of 1954—restricting the effectiveness of short-term trusts which revert to the grantor within ten years. These rules, however, do not apply to a trust that will last for the life of the beneficiary, and this is so no matter how short a life expectancy the beneficiary may have when the trust is created.

Temporarily, therefore—during the remaining life of his mother—Mr. Planner is permitted under the tax law to set aside a fund that will be treated as though it belonged, not to him, but to the one who receives the income from it. Although the income tax law does not specifically require it, Mr. Planner is careful to select an independent and unrelated trustee, such as a bank or trust company. Perhaps, if he named himself or his wife as trustee, the trust would "get by" for income tax purposes. But Mr. Planner's lawyer advised him not to go to the very limit of tax allowances, and in any event Mr. Planner wanted to get away from the task of remitting the money to his mother every month.

Gift Tax: The only gift represented by Mr. Planner's trust for his mother is a gift of the income from the property during his mother's life. There is no gift of the remainder, for the right to have the trust fund when the mother dies is retained by Mr. Planner himself. Obviously, a person cannot make a gift to himself.

Mr. Planner found that the value of his mother's life interest in the $50,000 amounted, under the Federal gift tax Regulations, only to about $10,000. A $3,000 annual exclusion would reduce the gift to $7,000; or, if Mr. Planner and his wife decide to "split" their gifts during the year, their two annual exclusions of $3,000 each would reduce the gift to $4,000. Mr. Planner and his wife had some of their $30,000 lifetime exemptions for the gift tax left, so there was no gift tax whatever to be paid on setting up the trust.

Estate Tax: A trust of this nature is not very effective in saving Federal estate tax. If Mr. Planner should die before his mother there would be included in his estate for purposes of the Federal estate tax the then value of the remainder interest in the trust. In view of the advanced age of the beneficiary, this remainder interest would come close to the total market value of the trust assets.

13

Take Out Insurance in Favor of Domestics

▶ *Under the inheritance tax laws of many States, life insurance payable to named beneficiaries is exempt. Another point: it may be easier to change the beneficiary under an insurance policy, if the beneficiary quits or dies, than to change the will.*

Very often a will leaves $1,000, $2,000, or $3,000 to each of several domestics in the testator's household.

Very often these gifts may be better accomplished by means of life insurance. A separate policy is taken out, by the testator on his own life, in favor of each of the beneficiaries. The advantages:

1. In some States the insurance proceeds will not be subject to a State inheritance tax. (A bequest in the will, of course, would be taxed, and the rate may be quite high inasmuch as the beneficiary is not a relative.)

2. The insurance arrangement is a private matter between the insured and his beneficiary. (The terms of a will are made public at the testator's death, and it would be unusual if every one of the domestics in the household should not be aware of the bequests to all the others.)

3. When a beneficiary dies or leaves his position it is a simple matter to surrender the policy for cash or change the beneficiary. (In a will it may be provided that a domestic shall have his legacy or bequest only if he is employed in the household at the testator's death. This, however, is not always a solution, for if an aged domestic is retired, his or her gift is cancelled—probably not as intended.)

A new employee in the household likewise might call for a change in the will, if gifts for others in similar positions are already set forth in the will. Or, if an employee dies and leaves a husband, wife, or other relative whom the testator wishes to have the gift, a change in the will may be required.

It is not always a simple matter to change a will. If the will is a long one, establishing trusts and other gifts for members of the family, the testator is likely to be disinclined to have a new will drawn every time a change is indicated with respect to gifts to domestics. The result, usually, is that faithful and deserving servants are left out and unintended beneficiaries are rewarded.

A change with respect to a single insurance policy, however, can be made without disturbing the arrangements made for members of the family and relatives.

Still another advantage, possibly, in providing for domestics by means of insurance lies in the optional methods of settlement. Under a $5,000 or $10,000 policy, for example, a straight life annuity for an aged beneficiary may be selected. But if such a beneficiary is provided for in the will, a small trust of $5,000 or $10,000 might be quite impractical.

"But I'm past the age for taking out life insurance," a man says when the idea of insurance for domestics is suggested.

Actually, life insurance is available to persons aged up to 65, and even beyond in some cases. The annual premiums are high, of course—high in relation to premiums on insurance taken out by younger persons. But they are not high in relation to the probable return from the policies. It would be sensible to pay the premiums on insurance for domestics from one's capital, rather than from income; and the "investment" of the capital in this way is likely to be as profitable as any other form of conservative investment.

14

Take Out Insurance Payable to Wife; Plus Testamentary Trust for Her Which Takes Out Insurance on Her Life

► *Wife spends capital from insurance, if it is payable to her under an annuity option. To re-build the estate, the trustee under her husband's will takes out insurance on her life, with children as beneficiaries. No estate tax at widow's death . . . No income tax payable by the widow. Yet her spendable income is almost as much as if she had income from entire estate.*

THE PROBLEM

With the aim of obtaining the full benefits from the estate tax marital deduction, a husband often leaves two trust funds for his widow, each for about half of his estate. One trust qualifies for the marital deduction and the other does not. Thus, only half his property is taxed when he dies (thanks to the marital deduction) and the other half is taxed when she dies later (the property in the trust that does not qualify for the marital deduction need not be taxed at her death).

Substantial tax economy usually results from this typical

"two-trust" arrangement for the widow. Note, however, these points:

1. Half the husband's property may be taxed when the widow dies.

2. The income from all the husband's property is taxed to the widow.

Can anything be done about these two points to bring even more tax economy to the two-trust idea?

SOLUTION

Here is a plan that might be considered jointly by the husband's lawyer and insurance underwriter.

Mr. Planner has $400,000, his wife has little or nothing. He takes out $200,000 insurance on his own life, paying for it from capital. For simplicity, we'll say this leaves him with an estate of $200,000, not counting the insurance.

He makes the insurance payable to his wife under a straight-life-annuity option. (This will qualify for the estate tax marital deduction.)

In his will he leaves his $200,000 estate in trust during the life of his widow, with instructions that the trustee take out as much insurance on her life as the trustee believes can be paid for with the income from the $200,000. If premiums should exceed income in any year, the difference is to be made up from principal; and if income exceeds the premiums, the excess is to be accumulated (or paid to the widow, in a State where accumulations for adult beneficiaries are not permitted).

The children are to be beneficiaries of this insurance taken out on their mother's life, and also remaindermen of the trust.

In most (though not all) of the States the husband would have to obtain the widow's consent not to "take against" the will, for she will not be getting much benefit, if any, from the estate that passes under the will. Moreover, the trust may or may not be valid in a limited number of States that do not, in general, permit accumulations of income for adult beneficiaries; the use of trust income to pay premiums on insurance may be regarded as a prohibited accumulation. (In New York, though, where accumulations for adults are not generally permitted, special legislation permits the payment of premiums.)

If such bars to the validity of the arrangement are not present or can be overcome, see what Mr. Planner has accomplished:

1. The annuity which the widow receives under the $200,000 insurance may compare favorably with the income she could receive from his entire $400,000 estate (as reduced by taxes and expenses at his death) if it had been left in trust for her.

2. The widow pays very little income tax on her annuity income. Also, her estate will not pay an estate or inheritance tax, nor will it be subjected to any estate-settlement costs.

3. The children eventually should receive close to $400,000, for the capital which the widow spends in the form of her annuity is largely made up by the insurance taken out on her life.

The ages of the husband and wife will have a bearing on the practicality of such a plan, as will also their insurability. Obviously, the plan could be suitable in only an extremely limited number of situations. But an estimate of the benefits from the plan is interesting, for a number of tax advantages inherent in life insurance come into play:

1. The husband makes a tax-exempt investment when he takes out the insurance. (For example, if premiums are $160,000 and the face amount of the insurance is $200,000, neither he nor anybody else pays an income tax on the $40,000 "gain.")

2. The income element in the widow's annuity is exempt from income tax up to $1,000 a year.

3. The trustee makes a tax-exempt investment when it takes out insurance on the widow's life, just as the husband did when he took out insurance on his life.

It is true that the trustee would be taxed for the income used to pay premiums or accumulated. If the widow should have any taxable income of her own, the taxation of income from half the husband's property to the trustee (rather than to the widow) could be advantageous. However, the trustee's income taxes could, possibly, be lowered or even eliminated entirely if the husband's will should direct the trustee to buy single-premium insurance on the widow's life. Thus there would be more insurance held by the trust (a tax-exempt investment) and fewer stocks and bonds producing taxable income.

15

Gift, with Donee Paying the Gift Tax, Saves Donor from Liquidating Assets

► *Donee borrows to pay the tax, then pays off the loan with income from the gift property. The amount of the gift, for gift tax purposes, is thereby lowered. Formula for computing the gift.*

Mr. Planner owned all the stock of a small company. He wanted his son to have an interest in the business, but he did not want to pay a gift tax . . . He just didn't have the cash.

"Let your son pay the tax on the gift," his lawyer advised him.

The idea was perfectly sound. Ordinarily, the donor pays the tax on a gift, but there is no reason why he cannot be reimbursed for the tax by the donee.

So Mr. Planner gave his son some stock. It was valued at $53,000. With the $3,000 annual exclusion taken off, the gift came to an even $50,000. Mr. Planner's gifts in excess of exclusions in earlier years had come to exactly $30,000, so he had no lifetime exemption left.

But was the amount of this gift to the son exactly $50,000?

No, because the son was going to borrow the money to cover the tax and was going to turn this money over to his father. (For simplicity, it is assumed that Mr. Planner here is a widower; or, if married, that he and his wife do not "split" their gifts for gift tax purposes in this particular year.)

The "clear" gift, then, was $50,000 less the tax. The real amount of the gift could not be computed until the amount of the tax was known. Just as certainly, the tax could not be computed until the amount of the gift was known. How did the son know how much money to borrow and turn back to his father?

First, he looked at the table of gift tax rates and guessed that the tax would be about $5,000. (It could not be more than $5,250, the tax on $50,000; and it could hardly be less than $3,600, the tax on $40,000.)

Second, he subtracted this assumed tax of $5,000 from $50,000, leaving an assumed gift of $45,000. Then he tentatively computed a gift tax on the $45,000. This tentative tax came to $4,425.

Third, he found the difference between the assumed tax ($5,000) and the tentative tax ($4,425). It was $575.

Fourth, he divided $575 by 1.165, getting $494. (The 1.165 figure is the rate of tax in the bracket in which the assumed gift falls . . . 16½%, expressed in decimals as .165 . . . plus 1.000.)

Fifth, he subtracted $494 from the assumed tax of $5,000. This left $4,506, the amount of the gift tax.

The son checked his computations by subtracting the tax, $4,506, from the $50,000, leaving $45,494 as the real amount of the gift. Then, from the table of gift tax rates, he found the tax on a $45,494 gift. It came to $4,506; so he knew he was right.

The son, of course, can take income tax deductions for the interest he pays on the $4,506 loan.

If the son ever sells his stock he will have a substantial capital gains tax to pay, for he takes as his basis, for computing gain, the same basis the stock had in his father's hands, which was almost nothing at all. The father and son, it might be thought, would do better if the father had kept the stock until he died and left it to his son by will. The son, in those circumstances, would have a stepped-up basis equal to the estate tax value of the stock. However, the other advantages of a lifetime gift outweighed the income tax consideration in this particular case, as they will in many similar cases. The son, not the father, was taxed for the dividends on the stock after the gift—a fact that saved Mr. Planner several thousands of dollars tax each year from then on. And Mr. Planner's probable estate tax was substantially reduced by the making of the gift, for the stock was completely gone from his estate. Finally, though it was not a tax consideration, the gift of the stock immeasurably increased the son's inclination to give his best efforts to the conduct of the business. As a partial owner of it, he was in a position to take over gradually the burdens of management as his father grew less active in the years ahead, and could keep the business going without interruption in the event of his father's death.

16

Generally, a Gift Should Not Be in Appreciated or Depreciated Assets

> ► *If assets have appreciated in value it may be better to hold during life and pass them on to the beneficiaries, by will, at stepped-up (estate tax) values. If the assets have depreciated in value, it is usually advantageous for the donor to sell them, obtain an income tax deduction for the losses, and then give the proceeds of sale to the beneficiary.*

APPRECIATED ASSETS

It is a surprising fact that many taxpayers do not realize there is no Federal income tax payable by anyone on the difference between the cost of an asset and its value at the owner's death. For example, a man paid $10,000 for some stock in 1935. He still has the stock in 1958, when he dies. It is then worth $30,000. The $20,000 "gain" is not reported on any income tax return—neither the owner's, nor his estate's, nor his beneficiaries'.

For estate tax purposes, the stock will be taxed at the $30,000 valuation. If the stock is later sold by the executor, or an heir, or the trustee of a trust under the will, the basis for computing gain or loss will be the $30,000 estate tax value. If, for example, the executor sells for $31,000, the gain will be only $1,000.

Now, if this man had given the stock to a member of his family shortly before he died, a sale by the donee at $31,000 would have resulted in a capital gain of $21,000, and the resulting tax might have been more than $5,000. Obviously, if a gift was to be made, it would have been advisable to select some other asset than this particular stock with its huge paper profit.

This rule holds true of gifts in trust as well as outright gifts. It matters not that a gift tax may have been paid, when the gift was made, on a valuation considerably in excess of the donor's cost. If the gift is ruled to be "in contemplation of death," thus being subject to a Federal estate tax, the trustee does become entitled to a stepped-up basis (value used for estate tax). But, of course, it cannot be known when the trust is created that it will come under the contemplation-of-death rule.

Appreciated property can, however, be put in a *revocable* trust. The creation of such a trust does not represent a gift subject to the Federal gift tax. The basis of the property, after the donor's death, is the estate tax value as used in his estate.

We are discussing, of course, non-charitable gifts. If the donee is a charity, or if a trust is being established with a charity named to receive the remainder, a gift in appreciated assets may offer pronounced advantages. *Reason:* The charity, or the charitable trust, will not pay an income tax on the sale in any event; and the donor's deduction for "contributions" is based on market value of the property at the time of the gift. A gift of appreciated property to a charity eliminates the income tax on the paper profit just as surely as does holding the property until the owner dies.

If appreciated property carries with it a latent income tax liability to the donee, can it be considered—for Federal gift tax purposes—to be worth somewhat less than current market values? The answer appears to be "No." The gift tax must be paid on full value, regardless of cost basis.

DEPRECIATED ASSETS

For computing loss on a sale of property received by gift, the donee takes the donor's cost *but never an amount in excess of value at date of gift*. Thus, if the donor paid $30,000, gives the property to someone when the value is $5,000, and the donee later sells for $5,000, there is no deductible loss.

Clearly, the donor would have been better off, taxwise, if he himself had sold the asset for $5,000 and then given away the $5,000 cash proceeds. He would have had a $25,000 deductible loss (subject to the usual limitations on capital-loss deductions). The advantage here in a sale by the donor would apply to gifts in trust as well as outright, and would also apply to both charitable and non-charitable gifts.

There is one consideration that partly offsets the advantage: a gift of depreciated property may be a little more valuable to the donee than cash, because if the property rises in value and then is sold by the donee there may not be a capital gain.

EXAMPLE: *Property cost donor $30,000. He gives it to donee when it is worth $5,000. Donee later sells it for $10,000.*

In these circumstances the donee would not have to report a capital gain. Having sold for less than the donor's cost (therefore no gain) and more than the value when received as a gift (therefore no loss), he has neither gain nor loss. If he had received $5,000 cash as a gift, invested it, and then sold the investment for $10,000, he would have had a $5,000 gain.

The taxable gain which the donee may escape in this way, however, can never exceed the loss that the donor would escape by selling the depreciated assets and making a gift of the proceeds.

17

Give Your Business to (1) Family and (2) Charity, at Same Time

> ► *A man owns all the stock of a company. Each year he gives some stock to members of his family and also gives some to a charity. The gift tax is balanced by the lowered income tax resulting from a deduction for the contribution. If the Government challenges valuation on the gift tax return, the business owner claims refund of income tax.*

Mr. Planner is president, director, and sole stockholder of a company. The company is an outstanding money-maker ... Mr. Planner's salary and dividends give him a taxable income of approximately $45,000, after deductions and exemptions ... but Mr. Planner knows very well that the company's earnings are largely due to his own talents and contacts. He does not believe that the company has any *transferrable* good will.

But will the Government believe this? His accountants and his lawyer warn him that, for gift or estate tax purposes, the company's stock might be valued far in excess of book value, for the earnings are huge in relation to the tangible assets.

This uncertainty as to valuation is troublesome to Mr. Planner. He wants to give the company's stock gradually to his three children (who are adults). He has been informed that he can give each of them $6,000 worth of stock—$18,000 altogether—each year without paying a gift tax. (He and Mrs. Planner would "split" the $6,000 gifts, so that each would report only $3,000—no more than the annual exclusion.) Gifts in excess of $6,000 to the children would require the payment of gift tax; both he and Mrs. Planner have used up their $30,000 lifetime exemptions and are, in fact, in the 8¼% gift tax bracket.

Despite the uncertainty as to valuation, Mr. Planner decides to go ahead with the annual gifts to his children. *But he also decides to give about $3,000 worth of the stock each year to charitable, religious, or educational organizations.*

Now suppose the Government does assert that the stock is worth considerably more than the book value at which Mr. and Mrs. Planner report the gifts on their gift tax returns. Here is what would happen the first year:

Gift tax and income tax results as reported on returns:

Gift to son A	$6,000	
Gift to son B	6,000	
Gift to son C	6,000	
Gift to charities	3,000	
Gift tax		$ –0–
Income tax saved by $3,000 gift to charities (Mr. & Mrs. Planner, on their joint return, are in the 59% income tax bracket)		$1,770

Results if Government should double valuation of stock:

Gift to son A	$12,000
Gift to son B	12,000

Gift to son C   12,000
Gift to charities   6,000
Gift tax ($18,000 gifts in excess of
  the annual exclusions, at 8¼% $1,485
Income tax saved by the $6,000 gift
  to charities (at 59%) $3,540

Mr. and Mrs. Planner would have to pay $1,485 gift tax. But they could claim refund of $1,770 income tax ($3,540 less $1,770).

The income tax refund would exceed the gift tax payable. Will the Government assert a higher valuation for the stock and attempt to collect a gift tax nevertheless? Mr. Planner will be satisfied if his valuation is allowed to stand. But if a higher valuation is sustained—that is, if the Government establishes that the company possesses transferrable good will and the stock therefore is worth more than its book value—Mr. Planner will continue making $6,000 annual gifts to each of his children (and $3,000 annual gifts to charities), with the shares valued, for gift and income tax purposes, at the higher figure.

In this way Mr. Planner expects to transfer, tax-free, a very considerable interest in his business within a period of ten years or so. ($18,000 a year for ten years is $180,000.) Not only will he be making his children part owners, giving them the incentive to take over the management of the business gradually as he retires, but he will also substantially reduce his taxable estate for estate tax purposes. He will also save income taxes, for the dividends will be split among him and his children instead of all being taxed to him.

Whether or not the valuation for the stock so established for gift and income tax purposes would carry over to the estate tax, if Mr. Planner should die, is uncertain. It may well be that the gift and income tax values would at least be a factor in determining the estate tax value. In any event, no better way of fixing the estate tax value appears to be possible, for a buy-and-sell agreement between father and children is not to be depended on in this respect. Usually, if a man wants his children to have his business some day, he must forego the attempt to "peg" the valuation for estate tax purposes.

Mr. Planner's annual gifts to his children and to the charity were outright. If the business owner's children are minors, the gifts might better be made in trust. A single trust could do for the children and the charity. For example, if Mr. Planner's three children were minors, he could measure the duration of the trust by the lifetime, until majority, of the youngest; with the income of the trust being distributed two-sevenths to each child and one-seventh to the charity. The principal of the trust at termination could be distributed in the same proportions. In these circumstances, one-seventh of the value of the stock added to the trust each year would be a deductible "contribution," and six-sevenths would represent gifts (largely, though not entirely, of present interests) to the children; so that if Mr. Planner should add $21,000 worth of stock in a certain year, he would get a $3,000 income tax deduction yet would pay very little gift tax.

18

What to Do about Jointly Owned Real Estate under the 1954 Tax Law

▶ *Husband buys real estate and puts it in his and wife's names jointly, with right of survivorship. The 1954 tax law does not require him to report the transaction as a gift. Nevertheless it might be to his advantage to do so.*

"We own our home jointly. It will pass to the survivor when one of us dies."

Many thousands of married couples say this. Joint ownership of the family residence has its disadvantages as well as its advantages; but there is no doubt that it is an extremely popular form of ownership.

In years prior to 1955 there has been a troublesome gift-tax complication connected with the arrangement. When one of the spouses—the husband, say—has bought the property with his money and registered it in his and his wife's names as "joint tenants with right of survivorship" or as "tenants by the entirety," he has been considered to make a gift, subject to the Federal gift tax, to the wife. Gifts have also occurred—technically, at least—every time he has paid off some of the mortgage, or when he has had improvements made to the property.

Probably the amount of the gift has not been large enough, in most cases, to require payment of tax. (There is a gift-tax marital deduction, a $3,000 annual exclusion, and also a $30,000 lifetime exemption from the gift tax.) But a gift tax return usually has been required, even where there was no tax payable. Needless to say, many taxpayers have been completely unaware that any kind of taxable gifts were being made, and they have unintentionally become delinquent in their tax liabilities.

The 1954 tax law eliminates this little "tax trap." It provides that, after 1954, no gift shall be considered to take place at the creation of the joint-ownership arrangement, or when a mortgage payment occurs, or when improvements are made—unless the spouse who paid most of the money elects otherwise.

If he does nothing—if he simply omits the filing of a gift tax return, for example—no gift-tax liability arises. Later, if the two owners should decide to "break up" the joint ownership arrangement, a gift would be considered to occur if the division of the property or the proceeds is disproportionate to the way they originally paid for it. But if the property is jointly owned until one of the spouses dies, there is never a gift tax.

This provision of the 1954 tax law applies to real estate held by husbands and wives as joint tenants with right of survivorship or as tenants by the entirety. It does not apply to real estate held jointly by other owners; nor does it apply to securities or other personal property, even if held by husbands and wives.

▶ Note that the above gift tax rule, dealing with jointly owned real estate of husbands and wives, is elective.

"Would it ever be to the taxpayer's advantage to have the transaction considered taxable at the start?" it may be asked.

Possibly there would be an advantage in some cases. Consider the hypothetical Mr. Planner. In 1955 he buys a house for $40,000, paying $20,000 cash. When he puts this property in his and his wife's names jointly with right of survivorship he may—if he files a gift tax return before April 15, 1956, and reports the gift—have the transaction treated as taxable immediately.

That is what Mr. Planner decides to do. But, actually, he does not need to pay a cent of tax. Why? Because the amount of the gift is less than his deductions and exemptions.

The amount of the gift is half, or approximately half, the $20,000 equity in the property. We'll assume the gift is correctly valued at $10,000.

Against this $10,000, Mr. Planner can apply a $5,000 marital deduction and also a $3,000 annual exclusion. This brings the gift down to $2,000. Mr. Planner has never used any of his $30,000 lifetime exemption, so of course the $2,000 is absorbed. $28,000 of the lifetime exemption remains.

In 1956 and later years Mr. Planner pays off some of the mortgage and makes a considerable number of improvements to the property. For each of these years he files a gift tax return; but, again, he pays no tax, for his deductions and exemptions are ample to cancel out the taxable gifts. In fact, in most years he finds he does not need to touch his lifetime exemption; the marital deduction and the $3,000 annual exclusion exceed the amounts of the gifts.

Now let's say that after 20 years the property is worth— not $40,000—but $90,000! Mr. and Mrs. Planner own it free and clear. They review their plans for the distribution of their property and decide that it would be better, for certain reasons, if this property were owned solely by Mrs. Planner, instead of by the two of them jointly. So Mr. Planner has it deeded to her.

The result is a gift by Mr. Planner to his wife of half, or approximately half, the $90,000 value.

But if Mr. Planner had not elected to have the transaction taxed at the start and as he added to its value in later years, the transfer to the sole ownership of Mrs. Planner would have represented a gift, for gift tax purposes, of the entire $90,000 value.

At the cost of merely the paper work involved in filing the gift tax returns, Mr. Planner substantially reduced a future gift tax liability. Not everyone will be so conscious of future tax problems as Mr. Planner; yet his plan does deserve consideration.

19

No Estate or Gift Tax
on $300,000 Estate

> ► *Gifts during life to wife and children cost noth-*
> *ing in gift tax (because annual exclusions, life-*
> *time exemptions, gift tax marital deduction,*
> *and the split-gift provision cancel out the tax-*
> *able gifts). The estate tax marital deduction*
> *then cancels out the taxable estate, leaving no*
> *estate tax to pay.*

In a message to Congress January 23, 1950, President Truman said:

> If a man leaves his estate of $300,000 at death, one-half to his wife and one-half to his three children, an estate tax of $17,500 must be paid. If his equally well-to-do neighbor gives away $180,000 to his wife and three children over a five-year period and leaves the other $120,000 at death, no estate or gift tax whatever is paid.

The President said this was an example of "excessive opportunities for tax reduction by splitting between the gift and estate taxes the total amount of wealth transferred by an individual." Congress, however, did not disturb those possibilities, and a married man with three children can still give, free of gift tax, as much as $180,000 to his family within five years as follows:

Gift (outright) each year—		GIFT TAX MAR. DEDUC.	ANNUAL EXCLUSIONS	"CLEAR" GIFT
to wife	$18,000	$9,000	$3,000	$6,000
to child "A"	6,000	--	6,000	--
to child "B"	6,000	--	6,000	--
to child "C"	6,000	--	6,000	--
Totals	$36,000			$6,000

The $6,000 "clear" gift could be applied against the husband's $30,000 lifetime exemption. It would be five years . . . after $180,000 had been given ($36,000 x 5) . . . before the $30,000 lifetime exemption would be used up. So no gift tax would be payable on the $180,000 total of gifts.

This would leave the husband with $120,000. If he left at least half of this by will to his wife his estate would get a $60,000 estate tax marital deduction. Then there would be the $60,000 exemption, so there would be no estate tax payable.

The wisdom of a husband's giving away so large a part (nearly two-thirds) of his property during his lifetime might be questioned. Purely from a tax standpoint, however, the plan is economical. Notice that the husband takes advantage of no less than five tax-relief provisions of the estate and gift tax laws:

1. *The Gift Tax Marital Deduction.* It reduced each of the yearly gifts to his wife from $18,000 to $9,000. (Such a deduction is allowed equal to half the value of gifts from husband to wife or wife to husband.)

2. *The Split-Gift Provision of the Federal Gift Tax.* Gifts, outright or in trust, by a husband or wife to a child

(or to anyone other than the donor's spouse) may be considered made half by the husband and half by the wife. Thus, when the husband in the example gave $6,000 to child "A," he and his wife were permitted to treat the gift as though he gave $3,000 and she gave $3,000.

3. *The Annual Exclusions for Gift Tax.* The first $3,000 given by any person to another during any year is not counted for gift tax purposes (unless the gift is a future interest). Thus, as to the $6,000 given to child "A," the half ($3,000) considered given by the husband is cancelled out by an annual exclusion and so is the half considered given by the wife.

4. *The Gift Tax "Lifetime Exemption."* Gifts by any person in excess of the exclusions are exempt up to $30,000. This is not an annual exemption, of course; it is allowed only once during the donor's lifetime. In the example, the husband's lifetime exemption saved the $6,000 "clear" gifts from being taxed during the first five years. If he should make similar gifts for a sixth year, he would have no more lifetime exemption left and he would be required to pay a gift tax on $6,000.

5. *The Estate Tax Marital Deduction.* This is allowed, up to half the adjusted gross estate of a married person, for the value of property left to the surviving wife or husband. In the example, this deduction ($60,000) brought the husband's $120,000 estate down to $60,000—no more than the estate tax exemption.

20

Tax on $600,000 Estate Cut from $187,000 to $92,000

► *$100,000 trust for children costs less than $1,000 in Federal gift tax. Estate tax on remaining $500,000 is $45,000, approximately, when husband dies and $45,000 when wife dies, if full use is made of the estate tax marital deduction. Total estate and gift tax, approximately $92,000, compares with $187,000 tax that could result from unplanned estate.*

THE PROBLEM

Mr. Planner had a $600,000 estate. He had made a simple will leaving the entire estate outright to his wife, and she had made a will leaving everything to the children.

He was shocked to learn that the probable Federal estate tax on his property would be $187,000—about $60,000 at his death and the rest at his wife's death later. With State taxes and estate settlement costs taken into consideration, less than two thirds of the estate would get to the children.

SOLUTION

By a change in his plans he reduced this probable tax to $92,000. Yet he did not need to sacrifice any of his objectives.

In short, the saving of about $95,000 cost him practically nothing. Here is what he did:

1. *He created a $100,000 irrevocable living trust for his three children.* Income was to be divided equally among them; and principal, when they died, would go to their children. For gift tax purposes, the gifts represented by the trust can be outlined like this, assuming Mr. and Mrs. Planner agree to "split" the gifts for gift tax purposes:

	TOTAL GIFT	MR. PLANNER'S SHARE, LESS $3,000 EXCLUSION IF PRESENT INTEREST	MRS. PLANNER'S SHARE, LESS $3,000 EXCLUSION IF PRESENT INTEREST
Life estate to child "A"	$ 20,000	$ 7,000	$ 7,000
Remainder after life estate	13,333	6,666	6,666
Life estate to child "B"	22,000	8,000	8,000
Remainder after life estate	11,333	5,666	5,666
Life estate to child "C"	24,000	9,000	9,000
Remainder after life estate	9,333	4,666	4,666
Totals	$100,000	$41,000	$41,000
Less lifetime exemptions		30,000	30,000
Net Taxable Gifts		$11,000	$11,000
Federal Gift Tax		$457.50	$457.50

The total gift tax payable thus would be less than $1,000.

2. *He leaves his remaining property ($500,000) in two trusts under his will for Mrs. Planner.* Each trust is for about half his estate. The widow is to receive all the income from each; but as to one of the trusts she has an unrestricted power to appoint the principal at her death, and as to the other trust she does not have such a power. The Federal estate tax results:

Husband's estate	$500,000	
Less marital deduction for property going into the power-of-appointment trust for wife	250,000	
His taxable estate, before the $60,000 exemption	$250,000	
Federal estate tax on his estate		$45,300
Wife's estate (the property in the power-of-appointment trust, if it is worth $250,000 at her death. The property in the other trust is not included in her estate.)	$250,000	
Federal estate tax on her estate		45,300
Total Federal estate tax, both estates		$90,600

Mr. Planner's arrangement of his estate saves $95,000 in Federal taxes. But it calls for setting up three trusts in all—a living trust for the children and two testamentary trusts for the widow. Are these trusts likely to have hidden disadvantages?

The fact is that the trust, apart from taxes, may be highly advantageous in conserving the property placed in them, and in freeing the beneficiaries from the worries and responsibilities of management. The widow, understandably, may have no experience in financial and investment matters. She probably would prefer to have the management of the property left to an experienced trustee. And as for the children, their trust constitutes an assurance that they will have incomes of their own—small incomes, it may be, but sure—regardless of the ups and downs of their father's business fortunes.

Trusts, if thoughtfully planned, not only save taxes but also make the property put in them last longer.

21

More Income to Widow if Remainder of Trust Goes to Charity

► *The charitable deduction reduces the Federal estate tax, leaving more property in the trust. Even more income may be available to the widow if half the husband's estate goes in a charitable-deduction trust, other half in a marital-deduction trust.*

Mr. Planner has a $400,000 estate. He has made a will under which his widow will receive the income for life from all his property.

Yet his estate will probably pay no Federal estate tax whatever!

How is this possible? It is explained by the fact that Mr. Planner's will creates two trusts for his wife, each for about half his estate. She is to receive all the income from both these trusts. Under one trust, the widow has an unrestricted power of appointment over the principal. The principal of the other trust is payable, at the widow's death, to a named charitable, religious, or educational organization.

The first trust—the one under which the widow has a power of appointment—qualifies for the estate tax marital deduction. Thus Mr. Planner's $400,000 estate will be cut to $200,000.

The other trust—which eventually goes to the charity—gives Mr. Planner's estate a charitable deduction of about $150,000. (The exact amount will depend on the wife's age when the husband dies.) Thus the $200,000 will be further reduced to $50,000.

That is less than the $60,000 estate tax exemption, so there will be no Federal estate tax.

The amount of the charitable deduction—estimated at $150,000 above—is the "present value," at the husband's death, of the approximately $200,000 that eventually will be received by the charity. Mortality tables in the estate tax Regulations enable that value to be readily computed. For example, if the wife is 72 when the husband dies, every dollar left in trust with income to her for life and with principal going to charity when she dies, represents a bequest to the charity valued at about 75¢. Therefore $200,000 left in such a trust represents a bequest of $150,000 (75¢ x 200,000).

To be certain that a deduction will be allowed his estate on account of the gift to charity, the husband should not give his widow the right to withdraw principal from the trust. He probably should not even provide that principal may be paid in the trustee's discretion for the widow's comfort, support, and maintenance. The possibility that principal might be diverted from the charity in this way could make the value of the gift unascertainable, with the result that no charitable deduction whatever would be allowed.

This does not mean, however, that the husband's plans must be inflexible. The widow's need for extra funds in an emergency could be taken care of by principal payments from the other trust—the marital deduction trust.

Notice that the charitable deduction in Mr. Planner's estate will not lower the top limit on the marital deduction. Both deductions are available, each without reference to the other. Here is an outline of the steps in bringing the $400,000 taxable estate (after deductions for debts and expenses) down to zero:

Gross estate		$450,000
Less debts and expenses		50,000
Adjusted Gross Estate		$400,000
(The charitable deduction is not taken off in arriving at the adjusted gross estate.)		
Less:		
The marital deduction (not more than half the adjusted gross estate)	$200,000	
The charitable deduction (the "present value" of the $200,000 eventually going to charity)	150,000	$350,000
Taxable Estate before Exemption		$ 50,000
Less the exemption		60,000
Taxable Estate		–0–

A plan such as this might be suitable even if there are children. An important point: the charity does not have to receive the $200,000 outright at the widow's death. The will could direct that the trust continue in perpetuity for the charity, and if the principal consisted of stock of a family corporation the children of the testator could participate in the management of the business.

The trust, for example, might hold preferred stock; the children the common (coming to them from the other trust under their father's will—the non-charitable trust); and the arrangement would be one of the best conceivable guarantees of the unified and continued operation of the business after the founder's death. Moreover, the usually troublesome problem of valuation of the stock in the father's estate would be greatly minimized, for every dollar of increase in valuation would mean only about 12½¢ in assets to be taxed (one quarter of the half of the estate going into the trust with charitable remainder).

22

It's Still Profitable to Create Living Trust for Wife

► *Man with $300,000 estate can save $21,000 tax by creating $100,000 irrevocable living trust for wife. Gift tax is low because husband and wife can "split" gift of the trust remainder.*

Before 1948 many husbands created irrevocable living trusts for their wives, with income tax and estate tax savings in view.

The 1948 Revenue Act, with its split-income and split-estates provisions, is popularly supposed to have put an end to the tax advantages in such trusts. Why divide the husband's income and property with his wife, if the effect of division can be obtained by filing joint returns (income tax) and by proper use of the marital deduction (estate tax)?

The fact is, however, that substantial tax savings can still result from irrevocable trusts created by husbands for wives. Here is a typical case:

A husband has $300,000; his wife has little or nothing. He puts $100,000 in irrevocable living trust, with income to wife for her life. When she dies, the trust ends and the property in it goes to their children.

The Federal gift tax (assuming the husband and wife have their $30,000 lifetime exemptions intact):

Gifts by husband . . .

(1) Life estate to wife	$50,000	
(Value of life estate, determined from tables in gift tax Regulations, depends on her age when trust created. In this case she is 52.)		
Less annual exclusion	3,000	
	$47,000	
(2) Half the trust remainder	25,000	
(Under the split-gifts election, husband reports only half the $50,000 gift to the remaindermen)		
	$72,000	
Less his lifetime exemption	30,000	
Husband's net taxable gifts	$42,000	
Husband's Tax		$3,930

Gift by wife . . .

Half the trust remainder	$25,000	
Less $25,000 of her $30,000 lifetime exemption	25,000	
Wife's net taxable gifts	–0–	
Wife's Tax		–0–
Total gift tax upon creating the trust		$3,930

The Federal estate tax:

Husband's estate, on an estate of approximately $200,000 with $100,000 marital deduction	$4,800
Wife's estate, on $100,000 received outright or in marital-deduction trust from husband's estate	4,800
Total Federal estate tax	$9,600

The total gift and estate taxes, if a $100,000 living trust is created, are $13,530.

If the husband does not create the living trust, and if he dies with an estate of $300,000, the total Federal estate taxes in his and her estates would be $35,000 ($17,500 in each estate), even with the best possible use of the marital deduction.

The living trust therefore results in a probable Federal tax saving of $21,470 ($35,000 less $13,530).

What if the wife dies first? In that case the probable saving of Federal taxes from the trust would be a little more . . . $23,670.

What if the husband dies before the wife but within three years after creating the trust, and the trust is held to have been created in contemplation of death? The tax saving in that case would be lost in this particular case. But there would not be a great "penalty." In other words, the taxes payable by the husband's and wife's estates would be very little more, if a trust is created and it is in contemplation of death, than if he had not created the trust.

In estates involving larger amounts than those shown in the example, there could easily be an advantage from the trust even though it should be in contemplation of death. That is because the payment of gift tax is, in a sense, a prepayment of the estate tax.

"But the remainder interest in a trust is a future interest," it may be said. "Can a husband and wife 'split' the gift of a future interest?"

Future interests, insofar as the Federal gift tax is concerned, are significant only in relation to the annual exclusion. A husband and wife may split gifts to third parties whether the gifts are present interests or future interests.

23

A Good Way to Leave Money
to Charity Is by Means
of Life Insurance

► *You can conveniently—and tax-economically—make a gift to a charity by making an insurance policy payable to it.*

A will isn't the only device for leaving property to a beneficiary when you die.

You can take out a life insurance policy on your life and make it payable to the beneficiary of your choice.

If it is a *charity* that you wish to benefit, an insurance policy has special advantages. With the payment of each premium, you have the satisfaction of knowing that you have put aside, in a sort of special fund, a gift that will live after you. This gift is independent of your will; it is unaffected by changes that you may make in your will, and the charity need not wait for the money while your estate is being settled.

Whether the charitable gift is by will or by insurance policy, it is free of Federal estate tax.

There may be a significant difference with respect to Federal *income* tax, however. Let's say the insured person assigns the policy to the charity, keeping no rights in it whatsoever. If he does so he gets a Federal income tax deduction for making a "contribution" equal to the value, if any, of the policy when assigned. Then, afterwards, he gets "contributions" deductions for the premiums he pays on the policy.

"Inasmuch as the charity will not receive the proceeds until many years in the future, does not the insured have to 'discount' the premiums in determining the amount of his 'contributions'?"

No, he does not. Remember, the charity will probably receive more than the total premiums paid on the policy. The proceeds of a whole-life policy exceed the aggregate premiums, if the insured lives his normal life expectancy. So, if he gets income tax deductions for the full amount of premiums, he is not getting more than he is fairly entitled to for the charity will eventually receive more than the amount deducted.

Of course, contributions are tax-deductible only up to 20% of adjusted gross income (or 30% in some cases).

Taxes Cut Down the Saving from Having Member of Family Serve as Executor

▶ *If the executor takes a commission, it is subject to income tax. If the executor does not take a commission, there is no estate tax deduction for executor's commissions.*

A man decided to name his wife to settle his estate. "It will save the executor's commissions," he thought.

As it turned out, his widow needed help at every step in settling his estate. The extra expenses that she incurred—over and above the expenses that an experienced executor would have found necessary—just about wiped out any saving of commissions.

In any case, only about 60% of the commission was "saved." She took her commission as executrix. It was taxable income, of course. Her top rate of Federal income tax was about 40%, so only 60% of the total remained.

"She should not have taken a commission," it may be said. But then there would have been no estate tax deduction for commissions paid. The top rate of estate tax was over 30%, so there would not have been much of an advantage, if any, in her giving up her right to a commission.

Moreover, would she have had to pay an income tax on the commission she could have drawn but did not? Conceivably, it might happen. The widow-executrix may be taxed, yet the estate may get no estate tax deduction.

▶ The whole question of executor's commissions is of little importance in estate planning. One of your *last* considerations, in selecting an executor, should be the cost in commissions. The services of an experienced, capable, impartial, and financially responsible executor are easily worth the commission he receives. Putting it another way, the damage done to an estate by an inexperienced or otherwise unsuitable executor can be ten times or more the amount of the commissions involved.

How a Family Corporation Can Make Estate Planning Easy by Issuing Preferred Stock

► Family corporation issues preferred stock as a stock dividend. Dividend is clearly non-taxable, under 1954 tax law. Owner of business then is in a position to (1) make gifts of preferred stock to family, (2) leave preferred stock by will to his widow, and (3) enter into buy-and-sell agreement covering the common.

THE PROBLEM

The typical business owner has most of his money in his business. If he does nothing about the problem while he is living, his estate may be caught in a tax squeeze.

The business may be valued for estate tax at an unexpectedly high figure (on account of good will); yet the business may be a poor source of cash to pay the tax, for the stock often is unsaleable except at sacrifice prices.

Mr. Planner owned all the stock of a small but prosperous company. The book value of the stock was $400,000. What would it be valued for estate tax purposes? Nobody could guess, for there was a big question about good will. Conceivably the Government would claim the company was worth a million dollars, for earnings in recent years had been substantial.

Mr. Planner had a wife and two daughters. There was no one in his family coming along to take over the business, so Mr. Planner considered a buy-and-sell agreement with his key employees.

But $400,000 was out of their reach. Even by taking out insurance on Mr. Planner's life they could not possibly raise more than $100,000 or so among them. And they were not interested in acquiring a minority interest, with Mr. Planner's widow holding the majority of the stock.

Then Mr. Planner considered gifts of some of the stock to his daughters and their husbands during his lifetime. In this way he could greatly reduce the probable estate tax on his estate. But such a plan was impractical, he decided, for he did not want to give up any control at all just yet. Moreover, the valuation problem would arise in connection with the gift tax, and the valuation of the stock he retained would still be a problem for his executors to face.

SOLUTION

Mr. Planner had his company issue to him, as a stock dividend, $300,000 of preferred stock.

The dividend was non-taxable for income tax purposes (see, on this point, section 305 of the Internal Revenue Code of 1954).

Then, from an estate-planning viewpoint, Mr. Planner was in a position to do these things:

1. *Create irrevocable living trusts for his two daughters, depositing some of his newly acquired preferred stock.* In

so doing he reduced his probable estate tax. He also saved income tax, for the dividends on the preferred would be taxed to his daughters thereafter and not to him. As for gift tax, there could not be much of a question as to valuation of the stock, for the dividends on it were fixed at 5% and each share would be entitled to assets at liquidation of the company only up to par value.

2. *Leave some of his preferred stock to his wife by will.* This would be a suitable investment for her (or for a trust created under his will for her benefit). The income yield was relatively high. And the preferred stock, giving a first lien on the company's earnings yet carrying with it none of the responsibilities of management, was made to order for absentee ownership. Moreover, valuation of the stock in Mr. Planner's estate for estate tax purposes would not be any more of a problem than was the valuation of the same class of stock for gift tax . . . It would have to be worth close to par.

3. *Enter into a buy-and-sell agreement, with key employees, as to the common.* The book value of the common was brought down to $100,000, approximately, by issuance of the preferred. This figure was within reach of the employees. Four of them took out insurance totalling $100,000 on Mr. Planner's life, and agreed to buy all the common stock from his estate at that figure. Mr. Planner, on his part, bound his estate to sell. Thus, with a trustee holding the stock and the insurance policies, this agreement gave as much promise of "pegging" the value of the stock for estate tax purposes as any such arrangement conceivably could. There was no doubt of its arm's length character; and the price—book value—was reasonable and fair to all parties.

Of course, the plan not only resulted in a big reduction of Mr. Planner's probable estate tax, but it also resulted in a great deal more liquidity in his estate. The $100,000 proceeds of sale of the common stock would be received by his executor within a matter of days after Mr. Planner's decease.

Last but not least, Mr. Planner retained full control over the management of the company during his lifetime. He had built up the business by a lifetime of hard work, and he could not consider relinquishing control of it to anyone else while he lived.

Mr. Planner's "perfect" arrangement will have a flaw in it for some business owners. It is the fact that the business owner may have started the company on a shoestring, and consequently the stock may carry a very low basis for income tax purposes. Now, if the business owner sits back and does nothing, merely holding his capital stock until he dies, his estate and his heirs will get—free of income tax—a stepped-up basis for all the stock, a basis equal to the values used for estate tax. If, on the other hand, the business owner goes through with the preferred-stock arrangement and puts some of the newly issued preferred in irrevocable living trusts for members of his family, he is in a sense perpetuating the low basis of the stock so transferred. (The trustee's basis for gain will be the same as the business owner's, even after the business owner's death. The basis may possibly be increased by the amount of Federal *gift* tax paid when the trust was created. This is a new rule added by the 1958 law.)

This is a matter to be carefully weighed. The disadvantage, however, will not apply to the common stock that is covered by the buy-and-sell agreement, for the estate is considered the seller of this, and the estate's basis is the estate tax value. Nor would the disadvantage apply to preferred stock which the business owner keeps and leaves to his family by will.

Another question to be gone into very carefully before the preferred stock is issued is the danger that the proceeds, if there is a sale or redemption later on, will be taxed as ordinary income (instead of as a capital gain). See, particularly, section 306 of the Internal Revenue Code of 1954.

Even if the business owner does not create irrevocable trusts and does not enter into a buy-and-sell agreement, the issuance of preferred stock still might greatly simplify the planning of his estate. He can, if he holds preferred and common, split up the ownership of his business in his will, giving his widow and daughters the preferred and his sons the common, for example. If there was nothing but the one class of stock—voting common—there might be marked drawbacks in having persons who would be inactive in the business holding large blocks of management shares.

Part Two

THE FEDERAL ESTATE
TAX IN OUTLINE

1

Some Facts about Estate Tax

▶ *The general nature of the tax. The exemption; the rates of tax. Relation to State taxes. Is your estate too small to be taxed?*

WHAT IS THE FEDERAL ESTATE TAX?

The Federal estate tax is a tax that your executor will have to pay on the property you own when you die, and on certain other property. Chapter 2 tells what this other property is.

Strictly speaking, the tax is not on the property itself but on *the transfer* of the property. The distinction is not very important if you are just making an estimate of tax.

IS THE TAX BASED ON MARKET VALUES?

Yes—on market values either at date of death or one year later. The executor has a choice between the two dates.

IS THERE A SEPARATE TAX ON EACH LEGACY?

No, there is only one tax no matter how many legacies there are. For example, if a man dies and leaves $150,000 to be equally divided among his three children, there will be one tax on the $150,000 estate. There will not be a separate tax on each $50,000 share.

WOULDN'T EACH CHILD'S SHARE OF THE ESTATE HAVE TO BEAR A SHARE OF THE TAX?

Perhaps. See Chapter 6, "Who Is to Bear the Burden of

the Tax?" But the thing to remember is that, though the tax may be split up and charged to several different legacies, it is still only one tax. All the property is lumped together, certain deductions are taken off the total value, and the balance is taxed.

IS THERE ANY EXEMPTION FROM THE TAX?

Yes, the estate of every United States citizen or resident has a $60,000 exemption. The exemption is classed as a deduction.

EXAMPLE:

Gross estate (market value of all property)	$150,000
Less deductions (debts, expenses, etc., and the $60,000 exemption)	80,000
Net estate (now called the "taxable estate")	$ 70,000

ARE THE TAX RATES APPLIED AGAINST THE TAXABLE ESTATE?

Yes. The rates are:

3% of the first $5,000
7% of the next 5,000
11% of the next 10,000
14% of the next 10,000

and so on, up to 77 per cent of amounts over ten million dollars. On a taxable estate of $70,000 the tax is $12,300.

Note: The "taxable estate," with the $60,000 exemption taken off, is an artificial figure. It does not correspond with the usual concept of a person's net wealth. Therefore estimates of estate tax are often made on the taxable estate *before* the exemption is deducted. A table showing the tax on taxable estates before the exemption is at page 267.

WHERE DO THE STATE INHERITANCE AND ESTATE TAXES FIT IN? CAN THEY BE DEDUCTED FROM THE FEDERAL TAX?

On a fairly large estate the Federal tax can be lowered by a credit for the State tax the estate must pay. The credit may not be more than a certain portion of the Federal tax, even though the State tax exceeds that portion.

EXAMPLE:

Federal tax on $70,000 taxable estate	$12,300
New Jersey inheritance tax, $2,350; maximum amount allowed as credit	240
Federal tax payable	$12,060

From here on, when we speak of the "Federal tax" we mean the net amount of Federal tax that is payable, after taking off the highest possible credit for State tax. In all States (except Nevada, which has no tax at all) the tax is at least as much as the highest possible credit.

AREN'T THE STATE TAXES PRETTY IMPORTANT TOO?

The State taxes are considerable in small estates because they generally allow small exemptions or else no exemptions at all. But the rates of the State taxes do not go up so steeply or so far as the Federal rates do. In medium-sized and large estates the Federal tax is much larger than the State tax.

HOW DO YOU FIND THE TOTAL TAX—FEDERAL PLUS STATE—PAYABLE BY AN ESTATE?

In all States except Nevada, simply add (1) the Federal tax as we compute it in this book and (2) the State tax.

EXAMPLE:

Payable to U. S. (Federal tax on $70,000 taxable estate)	$12,060
Payable to New Jersey (N. J. inheritance tax on $130,000 left to a son or daughter)	2,350
Total Federal and State taxes	$14,410

In Nevada there is only the Federal tax to be paid, but it is the Federal tax without any credit for a State tax. At page 267 there is a table showing this gross amount of Federal tax.

HOW MUCH TIME DOES THE EXECUTOR HAVE FOR PAYING THE FEDERAL TAX?

The general rule is that he must file a return and pay the tax within fifteen months after death. He may be able to get an extension of time. And if the estate consists largely of an interest in a business, the tax attributable to the business interest can, under certain conditions, be paid in 10 annual installments with 4% interest. (This rule was added in 1958.) But in most cases the tax is a liability that must be paid off with cash within the 15-month period.

HOW LONG HAS THERE BEEN A FEDERAL TAX?

Since 1916. It has been changed many times.

SINCE EVERY ESTATE HAS A $60,000 EXEMPTION, IS THERE ANY REASON WHY A PERSON WHO HAS LESS THAN THAT SHOULD BE CONCERNED ABOUT THE TAX ON HIS ESTATE?

Yes, there may be.

First of all, your "estate" may be larger than you think. At the start we said the tax was on the property a man owned *and on certain other property*. In the following chapter you will see that this "other property" may be your life insurance or property you own jointly with someone else or various other items of property that you may not ordinarily think of as being yours. Adding everything together, the total estate may be far greater than the exemption.

If you are in business, the government may put a value on good will or some other intangible. That may boost the valuation of your business, for tax purposes, to a far higher figure than you are counting on.

Finally, there is no guarantee that the estate tax exemption will stay at $60,000. In 1949 a bill introduced in Congress would have lowered the exemption to $30,000. In 1950 the President suggested that Congress look to the estate tax for additional revenues. Although these suggestions have not ripened into legislation, the exemption may eventually be set at a figure making the estate tax "everyman's tax." That is what happened with Federal income tax exemptions, which have been lowered to take in practically all of us.

2

Add Everything Together and Call It Your "Gross Estate"

▶ *The property that may be included in your estate for estate tax purposes: Real estate. Stocks and bonds. Mortgages, notes, and cash. Life insurance. Jointly owned property. Other miscellaneous property. Transfers while living. Powers of appointment.*

The tax is on the TAXABLE estate, which is what is left after deductions have been taken away from the GROSS estate.

Therefore, if you want to estimate the tax your estate will pay, the gross estate is your starting point. Here is the way the gross estate is computed on an estate tax return:

	VALUE
Real estate	$
Stocks and bonds	
Mortgages, notes, and cash	
Life insurance	
Jointly owned property	
Other miscellaneous property	
Transfers while living	
Powers of appointment	
Total gross estate	$

Let's consider these items in order. Make a rough estimate of your own gross estate as you go along.

REAL ESTATE

Generally speaking, include all your real estate.

But do NOT include real estate outside the United States. That is one of the very few things that is exempt from estate tax.

Do not include here the real estate you own jointly with someone else. It goes under "jointly owned property," farther down the list.

If your real estate is mortgaged, and if you are liable on the mortgage so that it could be collected out of your other property, include the real estate at its full value. There will be a place later on to take the mortgage as a deduction.

If you aren't liable on the mortgage and it is collectible only out of that particular piece of property, include in your gross estate only your equity.

Don't reduce the value on account of any dower or curtesy rights that your wife or husband may have under State law. The whole property must be included in your estate regardless of such rights.

STOCKS AND BONDS

Generally, include all your stocks and bonds. It doesn't matter whether an issue is foreign or domestic, or where the securities are kept. If you are a United States citizen or resident, they're all taxed.

Even so-called "tax-exempt" securities, such as State and municipal bonds, are subject to estate tax. There aren't any exceptions at all. Don't forget your United States Savings Bonds—they are fully taxed.

But do not include here the stocks and bonds you own

jointly with someone else. Put them under "jointly owned property."

If you are in business and the business is incorporated, this is the place to list the stock in your company. Do not depend entirely on book value. The government has the right to consider earning power, good will, and all other factors affecting value. Better discuss this question with your accountant or lawyer, but if you'd like to see just how the government thinks a business should be valued, see "Valuation of Closely Held Stock," at page 294.

MORTGAGES, NOTES, AND CASH

Include all mortgages, notes, and cash, except any that you own jointly with someone else. Cash means money in the bank as well as currency on hand.

Value mortgages and notes at less than face value if they aren't sound.

LIFE INSURANCE

"My insurance isn't payable to my estate. It will go direct to my beneficiary. That way I save the Federal tax on it."

Many persons have that idea. Unfortunately it is a mistaken idea.

► The correct rules are as follows:

1. If insurance on your life is payable to your estate, it will be included in your gross estate for Federal tax purposes.

2. Even if your insurance is not payable to your estate but is payable directly to the beneficiary, it will be included in your gross estate if you "own" the policy when you die—

that is, if you then hold an "incident of ownership" in the policy.

You are considered to own a policy if you possess *any* of the "incidents of ownership"—the right to borrow on the policy, for instance, or surrender it for cash, or change the beneficiary. Any one of these incidents of ownership makes you the owner, and can make the full proceeds of the policy includible in your gross estate.

Furthermore, the 1954 tax law—the "Internal Revenue Code of 1954"—specifies that the term "incident of ownership" includes a "reversionary interest" if the value of such interest exceeds 5% of the value of the policy immediately before the death of the insured. This new rule applies whether the interest arises by the express terms of the policy or by operation of law. What in the world is a "reversionary interest," you say? It's the possibility that the policy or its proceeds may return to the insured or his estate, or may be disposed of in some way by the insured. A possibility like this can be valued by actuaries. The method of doing so surpasses the understanding of most of us, but it seems to boil down to this: if you have better than 1 chance in 20 to get back the policy or its proceeds, then you are the "owner" of that policy for tax purposes.

Usually, where insurance has been taken out for family protection purposes, the person whose life is insured does own the policy in the sense that he can borrow on it, change the beneficiary, and so forth. Or perhaps he has a "reversionary interest." Probably, therefore, you will find you should include all your insurance in estimating your tax.

Of course, there are cases where policies will not be taxed. Sometimes it may be feasible to give away a policy—lock,

---

YOU CAN STILL PAY THE PREMIUMS

The estate tax rule used to be that insurance would be included in the insured person's estate if he owned the policy or paid the premiums. The premium-payment test was removed by the 1954 tax law. Thus, under certain conditions, the insured may now be able to save taxes merely by giving up all "incidents of ownership," even though he keeps on paying the premiums. More is said about this under the Tax-Saving Idea, "Assign Your Life Insurance," at page 16.

---

stock, and barrel—to the beneficiary, perhaps, or to the trustee of an irrevocable insurance trust. In that case the insurance ordinarily would escape being taxed in the insured's estate.

Keep in mind these exceptional situations. They may save taxes for you. But, as a broad, general rule, insurance carried by the breadwinner of a family is usually taxable in his estate.

JOINTLY OWNED PROPERTY

Like life insurance, jointly owned property is popularly believed to be exempt from estate tax. "It goes to my wife automatically," a husband says. "My will has nothing to do with it. So it's not a part of my estate."

The Federal tax rule is that it *is* a part of the husband's gross estate if he bought the property with his own money.

"At the most, only half the value should be included in my estate," the husband says.

He is wrong again. In figuring estate tax the entire value of the property will be included in his gross estate—unless his executor can prove that the wife contributed some of her own money toward the purchase of the property. By "her own money" we mean property that was originally hers, money that was not given her by the husband.

The burden of proof that such a contribution was made by the surviving owner is on the taxpayer. Very often the husband and wife do pool their money in buying the family home, or Savings Bonds, or some other item of property. But the job of tracing any part of the purchase price to either of them may, many years later, be just about impossible.

The law assumes that the one who dies first paid for everything. If you think your executor will not be able to upset this assumption with respect to your jointly held property, then you'd better include the full value in estimating your tax.

The bewildered husband's final argument is that he paid a *gift* tax when he had the property put in joint names, or when he paid off the mortgage, or when he made improvements. "They can't charge an estate tax and a gift tax on the same property, can they?" he asks. Indeed they can! It happens all the time. Perhaps some or even all of the gift tax can be used as a credit against the estate tax, so that there isn't always a double tax (more about this at page 142, Chapter 5). But, regardless of what went on as to gift tax, the property is at least included in the gross estate under the rules given above.

WHAT IS "JOINTLY HELD PROPERTY"? It is property of any kind that you and one or more persons own jointly with right of survivorship. If one owner dies, the survivor or survivors take all. You can't leave your share to someone in your will; your share automatically falls to the surviving owners, regardless of what your will says about it.

EXAMPLES: *Real estate held in names of two or more persons as joint tenants, or by husband and wife as "tenants by the entirety." Also joint checking accounts; and U. S. Savings Bonds registered in names of co-owners.*

But any property held by you and others as "tenants in common" is not jointly held property in this sense. Enter the value of your share of it under "real estate" or some other place, depending on what kind of property it is.

How to include less than full value: Suppose the property cost $10,000 and you paid $9,000, your wife $1,000. Do you merely take $1,000 off the date-of-death value and include the rest in your estate? No, you take off one-tenth of the date-of-death value. Remember that the date-of-death value probably won't be the same as the cost. What you do is reduce the value by a proportion—the proportion of the price that can be traced to the surviving owner.

What if the property wasn't purchased? Perhaps you and your wife, or you and your brothers and sisters, *inherited* some property jointly. Or you may have received it as a gift. In those cases, include in your gross estate half the value (if there are two joint owners), a third of the value (if there are three owners), and so forth.

OTHER MISCELLANEOUS PROPERTY

Include the value of debts due you and claims against others, household goods and personal effects, automobiles, and any other property you own that you haven't already listed.

ESTATE TAX ON PENSION & PROFIT-SHARING BENEFITS

Many employees participate in U. S. Treasury-approved pension or profit-sharing plans established by their employers. Suppose an employee does *not* contribute any of his own money to such a plan. Under the plan an amount—payable either in a lump sum, in installments, or as an annuity—goes to the employee's widow or other beneficiary at his death. Is the value to be included in the employee's estate for estate tax purposes?

Until the 1954 tax law was enacted the answer nearly always was "Yes." The 1954 law, in its provisions dealing specifically with the situation, generally exempts such amounts. This is a matter, however, that you had better ask your tax adviser about before definitely omitting the payments from your calculations.

If you are a farmer, include farm products and growing crops, livestock, farm machinery.

This is the place to include the value of your interest in a partnership or unincorporated business. Don't depend entirely on book value. The government has the right to consider earning power, good will, earnings expected from contracts already entered into, and all other factors affecting value. Better discuss this valuation problem with your accountant or lawyer. But whatever you do, don't be modest about the value of your business. If you are, you may underestimate your tax.

To be included here also is the value, at the deceased person's death, of payments that will continue for his widow or other beneficiary under a "joint-and-survivor" type of annuity. The valuation depends on the age of the beneficiary when the first annuitant dies, so of course it's a matter of guesswork if you have bought such an annuity and are now estimating your tax. Moreover, the general rule is that you need include only the fraction of the value that corresponds with the portion of the cost of the annuity paid for by you. Thus, if you paid half the cost and your wife paid half (and if your executor will be able to prove this), then only half the value of the continuing payments will be included in your estate for tax purposes.

TRANSFERS WHILE LIVING

Have you at any time made gifts of a material part of your property to your children, grandchildren, or others? Have you laid aside any of your property in a trust—a trust either for your own benefit or for others'?

If you have, then the property you have given away or the property in the trust at the time of your death may possibly be treated under the Federal tax law as though it were yours. In other words, the market value of this property perhaps will be included in your gross estate.

Briefly, here are the rules about these "transfers while living":

OUTRIGHT GIFTS: Money or property you have given away outright will be included in your gross estate if the gift was made "in contemplation of death."

For example, a man is worth $400,000. He is of advanced age and in poor health. To avoid estate taxes—or so he thinks —he gives $300,000 to his children. Upon his death shortly afterward there is little doubt that the government would say he was still worth $400,000; his $300,000 gifts were in contemplation of death and therefore, in figuring the tax on his estate, they should be added back to his other property.

▶ It wouldn't matter if he had paid a GIFT tax on the $300,000. There could be an estate tax on it too. However, as we shall see later, the gift tax might be used as a credit against the estate tax, so there wouldn't necessarily be a "double tax" on the $300,000.

Whether or not any particular gift is in contemplation of death is often a debatable question. But the Revenue Act of 1950 cleared away a great deal of the uncertainty. It provided that a gift shall *not* be considered made in contemplation of death if the donor lives at least three years after making the gift.

If the donor dies within three years of the gift, his executors will have the job of proving that contemplation of death was not the motive. In legal terms, there will be a "rebuttable presumption" that contemplation of death was the motive of the gift.

Here is a good rule to follow: If you are estimating your tax, be conservative and include in your gross estate all large gifts you have made to members of your family during the past three years. If you are considering making large gifts to your family, ask your lawyer how they would affect your estate tax.

TRUSTS: The property in a trust you have established might be included in your gross estate for several reasons.

First, you may have established the trust in contemplation of death. In putting property into a trust, you nearly always

THE RULE ON TRUSTS THAT "TAKE EFFECT AT DEATH"

If a trust "takes effect at death"—at the death of the person who established it—the property in it is taxable in his estate. The Internal Revenue Code of 1954 made a change in the Federal estate tax law on this point. The change was quite technical, but here is the general effect of it:

Have you established an irrevocable living trust under which property might come back to you or your estate if certain events should occur? If you have, and if your reversionary interest in the property just before you die can be valued at more than 5% of the value of all the property, then some or all of the trust may possibly be taxed in your estate as a transfer taking effect at death.

This is so—as to property put in such a trust anytime after October 7, 1949—whether the reversionary interest arises by the express terms of the trust agreement or, on the other hand, results merely from the inheritance or other laws.

Of course, there might be other reasons for taxing trusts like this. For instance, they might have been established in contemplation of death. The rule mentioned here deals only with the test of whether a trust takes effect at death.

are making a gift to somebody—to the beneficiary of the income, for instance, or to the persons who will eventually receive the principal. Like outright gifts, the gifts made by means of a trust may be in contemplation of death (if death occurs within three years of the gift). In that case the property in the trust would be included in your gross estate in figuring the Federal tax.

Second, you may have made yourself the beneficiary of the income, or you may have provided that at some future date the principal should come back to you or to your estate. Perhaps there is nothing more than the mere possibility that at some time in the future you or your estate will benefit from the trust and that possibility may depend to some extent on when you die. In any of these cases, some or all of the property in the trust may be included as a part of your gross estate.

Third, the trust may be "revocable," in which case all the property would be included in your gross estate. A revocable trust is one that you can revoke or change, or one as to which you can change the beneficiaries. If the trust was set up in recent years, it wouldn't matter whether you could exercise this control over it by yourself or whether you would have to get somebody's consent; in either case, the property in the trust would be treated—for estate tax purposes—as though it were yours.

These rules with respect to trusts have been briefly stated. If you have already established a trust, your tax adviser doubtless has advised you whether the property will be included in your gross estate. You should have him review the question occasionally, for tax laws change. If you are thinking of setting up a trust, you should discuss all aspects of the tax question with your tax adviser.

POWERS OF APPOINTMENT

Here is a typical power of appointment: John Jones receives a few thousand dollars a year from a trust fund set up several years ago by his grandfather. The income will continue as long as John Jones lives. At his death the trust is to end and the principal is to be turned over to anybody he cares to give it to in his will.

Actually it isn't John Jones who gives this money away.
is—or, rather, it was—his grandfather. All that Jones does
is to name the persons to receive it. In other words, he "appoints" it. He has a "power of appointment."

▶ If Jones leaves a valid will and appoints the fund to
someone, the market value of the whole fund will be included in his gross estate for Federal tax purposes.

MERE POSSESSION OF POWER MAY CAUSE TAX: What if Jones
decides not to appoint the fund to anybody? Perhaps the
fund is slated to go to his children, in the event he does
nothing. So why can't he just sit back and let the children
have it—and in this way save tax?

Unfortunately, there might not be a saving. The rule is
that mere possession of the power would cause the fund to
be included in his gross estate *if the grandfather established
the fund after October 21, 1942.*

Only if the grandfather created the power of appointment
on or before October 21, 1942, could Jones save estate tax by
refraining from exercising the power. Of course, Jones will
think twice before taking this means of saving tax. If, under
the grandfather's will, the property would go to someone
Jones thinks should not have the money, Jones would probably step in and name his own beneficiaries, tax or no tax.

WHEN A POWER IS "CREATED": If the person who left a will
containing a power of appointment died on or before October 21, 1942, it is clear that the power was "created" on or
before that date. If he died after that date but before July 1,
1949, the law says the power may be considered created on
or before October 21, 1942, if the will was dated on or before

October 21, 1942, and was not changed, by codicil or otherwise, afterwards.

Of course, a power of appointment could be created by a living trust agreement, or possibly by an insurance policy, as well as by a will. The law has nothing to say about when such a power is created. Possibly, if the instrument is "revocable," the power is not to be considered created until the grantor dies or gives up his right to revoke.

"LIMITED" POWER OF APPOINTMENT: In the example of a typical power of appointment, Jones had a "general" power. That is, he could name anyone at all to receive the fund at his death. He could even name his own estate or his creditors.

But if his grandfather's will provided that he should not have the right to appoint the property to himself, his estate, or the creditors of himself or his estate, he would have a "limited" power of appointment. In that case the trust would not be included in his estate for Federal estate tax purposes even if he should exercise the power; and this would be so regardless of when the trust was created.

EXAMPLE: *Jones, who receives the income for life from the trust under his grandfather's will, may name anyone at all to receive the property in the trust when he dies . . . except that he may not have the property go to himself, his estate, or the creditors of himself or his estate.*

Even if Jones makes a will directing that the property in the trust shall pass to his children in certain proportions, the property will not be taxed in his estate.

Thus, a "limited" power of appointment can be quite broad, giving the holder of the power just about as much control over the disposition of the property as he could ever want. But, since it is not quite the complete control that would exist if the holder could take the property himself while living, or have it go to his estate or the creditors of himself or his estate, it results in no estate tax liability when the holder dies.

THE LAW: These rules as to the taxation of powers of appointment were put in the tax law in 1951. They are now contained in sections 2041 (estate tax) and 2514 (gift tax) of the Internal Revenue Code of 1954. These sections in their entirety should be referred to by anyone interested in the more technical aspects of releases, exercises, etc., of powers. Just to help you keep the more important points straight, here is a brief summary of the estate tax rules:

TYPE OF POWER AND WHAT YOU DO WITH IT	IS THERE AN ESTATE TAX?	REMARKS
If you have a *general* power created *on* or *before* Oct. 21, 1942, and you . . .		
—exercise it by will	Yes	Tax applies to "any property with respect to which" the power is exercised. There would be a tax, therefore, even though the beneficiaries you name in exercising the power may be the same persons who would get the property if you refrained from exercising it.

—have it when you die but do not exercise it	No	This is a perfectly valid way to save tax. Make sure, however, that your will does not *unintentionally* exercise the power.
If you have a *general* power created *after* Oct. 21, 1942, and you . . .		
—exercise it by will	Yes	Tax applies to "any property with respect to which the decedent has at his death" a power.
—have it when you die but do not exercise it	Yes	Tax applies to "any property with respect to which the decedent has at his death" a power.
If you have a *limited* power, whenever created, and you . . .		
—(1) exercise it by will, or (2) have it when you die but do not exercise it	Generally, no tax	Possible exceptions would be where the limited power is what remains after a general power has been partially released; or where (in one State, at least) a "new" limited power is exercised by giving someone else a power of appointment over the property.

3

Take Off Your Deductions

► *Your estate tax deductions: The exemption.
Funeral and administration expenses. Debts.
Mortgages and liens. Net losses. The marital
deduction. The charitable deduction.*

Here is a list of the items you can deduct from your gross
estate:

	AMOUNT
The exemption	$ 60,000
Funeral and administration expenses	
Debts	
Mortgages and liens	
Net losses while the estate is being settled	
The marital deduction	
The charitable deduction	
Total deductions	$

Write down an estimate of your deductions. The following comments may help you.

THE EXEMPTION

The estate of every United States citizen or resident is entitled to an exemption of $60,000.

That means that if your gross estate is less than $60,000,
your estate will pay no tax.

Even if your gross estate is more than $60,000, your estate

124

will not necessarily pay a tax. For instance, your gross estate might be $80,000. If your estate had as much as $20,000 of other deductions (for debts, expenses, charitable bequests, etc.), the total deductions, including the exemption, would be $80,000, leaving nothing to be taxed.

FUNERAL AND ADMINISTRATION EXPENSES

This item can be thought of as having four parts:
1. Funeral expenses
2. Executor's commissions
3. Attorney's fees
4. Miscellaneous expenses of settling the estate

If your estate is $50,000 or more, the cost of (2), (3), and (4), together, might be around 7 or 8 per cent of the value of the property passing into the hands of your executor. Funeral expenses include any proper payments by the executor for a burial plot and tombstone.

All you can do is make a rough estimate. Don't estimate too high, for if you do you will underestimate your tax.

DEBTS

This means *unsecured* debts and claims. If you owe money on a mortgage or collateral loan, it goes under the next following item, "mortgages and liens."

Any unpaid Federal and State income taxes on income up to date of death are deductible here.

MORTGAGES AND LIENS

In figuring your gross estate in the preceding chapter, did you include the *full value* of any real estate or other assets

---

WATCH OUT FOR "PROHIBITED TRANSACTIONS"

The Revenue Act of 1950 closed a number of loopholes in the tax laws. One of these was supposed to be in connection with charitable, etc., trusts. It was thought that some people have put money in these trusts—and have been allowed tax deductions for doing so—and then have been granted special favors of one kind or another by the trusts. So the 1950 act "prohibited" transactions in which a trust

1. lends any part of its income or principal (set aside for a charity, etc.) without adequate security or at an unreasonable rate of interest to donors, members of their families, or a corporation which they control;

2. pays any compensation to such persons other than a reasonable allowance for personal services actually rendered;

3. makes any part of its services available to such persons on a preferential basis;

4. makes any substantial purchase of securities or other property from such persons for more than an adequate consideration;

---

that you have mortgaged or pledged to secure a loan? If you did, then here is the place to deduct the amount you owe.

Do not deduct anything else here. For instance, do not deduct the amount owing on a mortgage on real estate outside the United States. Such real estate is not included in your gross estate, so it would probably be held unfair to take a deduction for the mortgage.

NET LOSSES WHILE THE ESTATE IS BEING SETTLED

Do not deduct anything here. This item covers losses from

5. sells any substantial part of its securities or other property to such persons without adequate consideration; or

6. engages in any other transaction which results in a substantial diversion of its income or principal (set aside for a charity, etc.) to such persons.

Under the law as it stands now, tax deductions are not generally allowed for gifts or bequests to a trust that engages in "prohibited transactions." Furthermore, the trust itself may be penalized by the loss of deductions. So when setting up a charitable, etc., trust, make sure that no such transactions will ever be possible.

(It is quite all right, however, to use the trust to perpetuate your name or the name of a member of your family. For example, a trust under the will of John Jones could provide an annual "John Jones Scholarship." That would not be a prohibited transaction.)

The rule about prohibited transactions applies to a few classes of tax-exempt corporations and associations, as well as to trusts. Special favors to donors or to their families may result in the loss of valuable tax deductions.

---

fire, storm, or some other casualty, or from theft. Obviously you can't know there will be any losses like that.

THE MARITAL DEDUCTION

If you are not married, you can't deduct anything under this item.

If you are married, your estate may have a large marital deduction. It is explained in the following chapter. Leave this item blank until you have read the explanation.

THE CHARITABLE DEDUCTION

If a charitable organization receives, say, $10,000 under the terms of your will, the $10,000 is an allowable deduction in figuring your taxable estate.

That's a simple example of a charitable deduction. But it doesn't tell the whole story. The estate tax law says an estate can deduct the amount of bequests, etc.:

(1) to or for the use of
    —the United States, any State, Territory, any political subdivision thereof, or the District of Columbia,
    for exclusively public purposes;

(2) to or for the use of
    —any corporation organized and operated exclusively for religious, charitable, scientific, literary, or educational purposes (including the encouragement of art and the prevention of cruelty to children or animals),
    if no part of the net earnings of the corporation inures to the benefit of any private stockholder or individual, and no substantial part of the activities of which is carrying on propaganda, or otherwise attempting to influence legislation;

(3) to
    —a trustee or trustees, or a fraternal society, order, or association operating under the lodge system,
    if such contributions or gifts are to be used by such trustee, trustees, fraternal society, order, or association exclusively for religious, charitable, scientific, literary, or educational purposes, or for the prevention of cruelty to children or animals, and no substantial part of the activities of such trustee or trustees, or of such fraternal

---

DELAYED PAYMENTS TO CHARITY

Suppose your will leaves $100,000 in trust for a member of your family. He or she is to have the income for life, and then the principal is to be turned over to a charity. Will your estate get a charitable deduction? YES, because the money will surely go to the charity someday. Will the deduction be $100,000? NO, because the payment is delayed. It must be discounted according to a mortality table in the estate tax Regulations. This table is shown at page 271, and the subject of delayed gifts to charity is treated in detail in Chapter 16.

(Payment of income to a member of the family in this situation is not a prohibited transaction of the kind explained on page 126. The *income* has not been set aside for charity. It is only the funds that are held or have been set aside for the charity—the *principal* in this case—that are protected by the prohibited-transaction rule.)

---

society, order, or association, is carrying on propaganda, or otherwise attempting to influence legislation; or
(4) to or for the use of
—any veterans' organization incorporated by Act of Congress, or of its departments or local chapters or posts, no part of the net earnings of which inures to the benefit of any private shareholder or individual.

The word "charitable," it will be seen, is shorthand. In tax circles it is used to describe gifts for religious, scientific, literary, or educational purposes as well as charitable purposes. It even covers gifts to the Federal and local governments.

Notice that the money doesn't have to go to an already-established organization. You can set up your own corporation or association by detailed instructions in your will, if you want to; or you can direct that the money be held in trust, with the trustee paying out the income for a specified charitable purpose.

Notice, too, that there is no limit on the deduction, like there is on the "contributions" deduction on your Federal income tax return. You could give all your estate to charity (if that's permissible under the law of your State) and perhaps wipe out your estate tax entirely.

Still another point: the money or property going to the charity doesn't have to pass under your will. For example, you might have a life insurance policy with a charity named as the beneficiary. For estate tax purposes, the proceeds of the policy will be included in your gross estate, if you own the policy. But those proceeds will come right out again as a charitable deduction.

4

The Marital Deduction

> ▶ *What the marital deduction is and what it can do for your estate. The top limit—half the "adjusted gross estate." How to leave the property, if you want the deduction for your estate.*

The "marital deduction" is relatively new. It was added to the estate tax law by the Revenue Act of 1948.

WHAT IT IS AND WHAT IT DOES

The deduction is allowed for the value of property that a married person leaves to his wife or husband.

It is something like the charitable deduction. The charitable deduction is given if property is left to a charity. The marital deduction is given if property is left to a spouse.

But there's a top limit on the marital deduction. It can't be more than roughly half your estate.

That means you can't always wipe out your tax just by leaving property to your wife or husband. Sometimes you can. For instance, a man is worth $100,000 when he dies. His will leaves $50,000 or more to his wife. His marital deduction, therefore, is $50,000, bringing his estate down to less than the $60,000 exemption.

If a man is worth, say, $300,000, the most he can do by leaving property to his wife is to bring his estate down to

$150,000 (because the deduction can't be more than about half the estate). With the $60,000 exemption taken off, $90,000 remains to be taxed.

He wouldn't wipe out his tax. BUT HE WOULD CUT IT BY MUCH MORE THAN HALF. The tax on a $300,000 estate without a marital deduction is $59,100; with the largest possible deduction it is $17,500.

▶ The big drop is due to the fact that the marital deduction—or any other deduction, for that matter—comes "off the top" of the estate, where the rates are highest. If you cut the estate in half, you always reduce the tax by more than half.

The marital deduction, therefore, is extremely important. It may be much more than all your other deductions put together. It may save many thousands of dollars tax in your estate. Make sure, by reading the rest of this chapter, that you understand it.

THE KEY QUESTIONS

In making an estimate of your tax, there are two questions you will want answered:

First, exactly what is the top limit on the marital deduction? We said it is "roughly half the estate." Half of the gross estate, the net estate, or what? If you are leaving the bulk of your property to your wife or husband, you can be pretty sure your estate will get the maximum deduction; but what's the maximum?

Second, HOW must the property be left to the wife or husband? Must it be left outright, or can it be left in trust?

Must it be left under the will? Or, does life insurance payable to the spouse count toward the deduction? What about jointly held property—is it considered "left to" the surviving owner?

With the answers to these two questions, you will be prepared to figure the marital deduction in your estate. Whether it is best for you to have the biggest possible deduction is something else again. In saving tax in your estate, you may be adding to the tax in your wife's or husband's estate. That is a matter to be discussed in Chapter 14. Right now the problem is to find the amount of the marital deduction in your estate under your present arrangements.

THE TOP LIMIT

The marital deduction can never be more than half the "adjusted gross estate."

The adjusted gross estate is the gross estate less

Funeral and administration expenses	$
Debts	
Mortgages and liens	
Net losses while estate is being settled	
Total	$

Subtract the above total from your gross estate, divide the remainder by two, and you have the maximum marital deduction in your estate.

Anything you leave your wife or husband up to that maximum is deductible. If you leave your wife or husband more than the maximum, only the maximum can be deducted.

COMMUNITY PROPERTY: If you and your present wife or husband own "community property," or if you once owned some, there is a special rule for figuring the top limit on the marital deduction in your estate.

Briefly, the special rule where there is or has been community property is this: To figure your adjusted gross estate, you subtract from your gross estate

(1) the value of your interest in community property;

(2) the value of your separate property that you got in a split-up of community property, if you got half or less as your share (if you got more than half there's a formula for finding how much to subtract);

(3) life insurance included in your gross estate if you paid for it with community property or with separate property as described above;

(4) transfers while living included in your gross estate if the property transferred was community property or was separate property as described above; and

(5) the part of debts, expenses, etc., in your estate that is *not* attributable to community property or to separate property as described above.

The net effect of these rules in most cases is that if a husband and wife in Texas, say, or California, have nothing but community property, the one who dies first cannot possibly get a marital deduction for his estate (because his "adjusted gross estate" will be zero). If a man has some separate property in addition to his interest in the community property, he may get a marital deduction for his estate in an amount up to one-half the value of his separate property.*

---

* Assuming he leaves his spouse property amounting to at least half the value of his separate property. But the property so left, to qualify for the marital deduction, may be either separate property or his interest in community property.

HOW TO LEAVE THE PROPERTY

If you leave $10,000 to your wife or husband outright, with no strings attached, your estate is entitled to a marital deduction for the $10,000 (so long as this plus the value of other property going to the spouse isn't more than the top limit on the deduction).

That is so whether the $10,000 goes under your will or as life insurance proceeds or in any one of several other ways.

But if you try to tie up the money so that your wife or husband doesn't have the full benefit of it, then your estate may possibly lose the deduction.

The following table shows the more common ways you can leave property to your wife or husband. "Yes" means your estate will get a deduction for the value of the property so left. (But keep in mind the top limit.) "No" means your estate won't get a deduction.

METHOD	DEDUCTION?
Outright bequest under your will	Yes
By intestacy (your spouse's legal share of the estate if you leave no will)	Yes
In trust under your will, spouse has all the income for life and has the unrestricted right to name the persons to receive the principal afterward (In a trust like this it wouldn't matter if the trustee had the right to pay principal to the spouse in emergencies. But the trustee must not have the right to pay principal to anybody else.)	Yes

METHOD	DEDUCTION?
In a trust like the one above, except that the spouse will lose the income upon re-marriage	No
In trust under your will, spouse has the income for life but has no rights in connection with the principal	No
By a trust made during your life that is included in your gross estate because it is revocable, "in contemplation of death," or for some other reason; and that gives your spouse all the income for life (after your death) plus the unrestricted right to name the persons to receive the principal afterward	Yes
By a "legal life estate" (for example, a farm), where the spouse has not only the income for life but also the unrestricted right to name the persons to receive the property afterward	Yes
By an insurance policy on your life (assuming the proceeds will be included in your gross estate) if	
1. the proceeds are payable to your spouse in a lump sum	Yes
2. the proceeds are kept on deposit with the insurance company at interest, your spouse getting the interest at least annually and having the right to withdraw the principal	Yes

METHOD   DEDUCTION?

(Instead of the right to withdraw
principal, the spouse could have the
right to have it paid to her estate at
death; or the principal could be payable to her estate in any event.)

3. the proceeds are payable in the form   **Yes**
of an income to your spouse for life and
at least for 10 years, 20 years, or some
other guaranteed period; and the spouse
has the right to take the value of the
remaining payments in one lump sum at
any time
  (Instead of the right to take the value
  of the remaining payments, the spouse
  could have the right to make any
  amount that may be due after her
  death payable to her estate; or such
  amount could be payable to her estate
  in any event.)

4. the proceeds are payable to the spouse   **Yes**
in installments for a certain period or in
certain amounts, and the spouse has the
right to take the value of the remaining
payments in one lump sum at any time
  (Instead of the right to take the value
  of the remaining payments, the spouse
  could have the right to make any
  amount that may be due after her
  death payable to her estate; or such
  amount could be payable to her estate
  in any event.)

METHOD	DEDUCTION?
5. the proceeds are payable to an insurance trust, with your spouse having the rights as to income and principal that are necessary for the deduction in the case of a trust under your will	Yes
You and your spouse own a house, Savings Bonds, or any other property as joint tenants or tenants by the entirety; you die and the whole property goes to your spouse	Yes, to the extent the property is included in your gross estate for tax purposes
You buy an annuity for yourself and your spouse; you die and the payments continue for the spouse, with no possibility of payments to anyone else	Yes, to the extent of the value of the annuity at your death

5

How to Estimate the Tax
Your Estate Will Pay

▶ *Your taxable estate. Rates of tax on the tax-*
able estate. Credits against the tax.

YOUR TAXABLE ESTATE

Subtract from your gross estate (Chapter 2) $
your deductions (Chapter 3)

and get your TAXABLE ESTATE $

THE RATES

Find your tax by applying the following rates against your
taxable estate:

(1) TAXABLE ESTATE	(2) TAX ON AMOUNT IN COLUMN (1)	(3) RATE OF TAX ON NEXT BRACKET (PER CENT)
$ —	$ —	3
5,000	150	7
10,000	500	11
20,000	1,600	14
30,000	3,000	18

(1)	(2)	(3)
TAXABLE ESTATE	TAX ON AMOUNT IN COLUMN (1)	RATE OF TAX ON NEXT BRACKET (PER CENT)
40,000	4,800	21.2
50,000	6,920	24.2
60,000	9,340	27.2
90,000	17,500	26.4
100,000	20,140	28.4
140,000	31,500	27.6
240,000	59,100	26.8
250,000	61,780	28.8
440,000	116,500	28.0
500,000	133,300	31.0
640,000	176,700	30.2
750,000	209,920	32.2
840,000	238,900	31.4
1,000,000	289,140	33.4
1,040,000	302,500	32.6
1,250,000	370,960	35.6
1,500,000	459,960	38.6
1,540,000	475,400	37.8
2,000,000	649,280	41.8
2,040,000	666,000	41.0
2,500,000	854,600	45.0
2,540,000	872,600	44.2
3,000,000	1,075,920	47.2
3,040,000	1,094,800	46.4
3,500,000	1,308,240	49.4

TAXABLE ESTATE	(2) TAX ON AMOUNT IN COLUMN (1)	(3) RATE OF TAX ON NEXT BRACKET (PER CENT)
3,540,000		
4,000,000	1,328,000	48.6
4,040,000	1,551,560	52.6
5,000,000	1,572,600	51.8
5,040,000	2,069,880	55.8
	2,092,200	55.0
6,000,000		
6,040,000	2,620,200	58.0
7,000,000	2,643,400	57.2
7,040,000	3,192,520	60.2
8,000,000	3,216,600	59.4
	3,786,840	62.4
8,040,000		
9,040,000	3,811,800	61.6
10,000,000	4,427,800	60.8
10,040,000	5,011,480	61.8
	5,036,200	61.0

For example, suppose your taxable estate is $100,000. Your tax is $20,140.

If your taxable estate is $108,000, your tax is

$20,140 (the tax on $100,000), plus
 2,272 (the tax on the next $8,000 @ 28.4%), or
$22,412 (the total tax).

Remember that these are the rates of your Federal tax—the net Federal tax that is payable after the highest possible credit for State tax has been taken off. The State tax is always as much as, or more than, the maximum credit (except in Nevada, where there's no State tax at all); so the above rates give a true picture of what most estates must turn over to the Federal tax authorities.

CREDITS AGAINST THE TAX

Some estates, however, are entitled to an additional credit —or even two additional credits. Their Federal tax is figured according to the above rates. Then the tax is reduced by a credit for

1. Federal GIFT TAX that may have been paid on property that is subject also to the estate tax, or
2. Federal ESTATE TAX paid on PRIOR TRANSFERS, or
3. both.

The two credits are often confused. No. 1, the credit for gift tax, arises from this situation: Mr. A gives property away while he is living—to his wife or children, for instance. He pays a Federal gift tax at that time. Nevertheless, the very same property may be included in Mr. A's estate for Federal estate tax purposes—because, for example, the gift is held to have been made "in contemplation of death." To prevent hardship, the estate tax law allows the tax on Mr. A's estate to be reduced by all or some part of the gift tax that he paid earlier.

No. 2, the credit for estate tax paid on prior transfers, is likewise a relief provision. It comes into play where successive deaths occur within a relatively short period. For example, Mr. A dies in 1954, leaving all his estate to Mr. B. Mr. B dies in 1955. Mr. B's estate—the "second" estate, it is called in tax circles—is entitled to a credit for all or some part of the estate tax paid by Mr. A's estate.

No. 1, the credit for gift tax, results only where the decedent has given away property.

No. 2, the credit for estate tax paid on prior transfers, results from just the opposite situation—where the decedent has *acquired* property.

AMOUNT OF CREDIT FOR GIFT TAX: The credit for gift tax is allowed in the amount of gift tax that was paid, *except that it may not be more than the amount of estate tax that is attributable to the gift.*

The exception sometimes cuts the credit down to a fraction of the gift tax that was paid.

EXAMPLE: *An unmarried man gives away $100,000 worth of property in contemplation of death. He pays $9,000 gift tax. When he dies the property has dropped in value to $40,000.*

Assume his entire estate, including the $40,000 of property he had given away, is $160,000 (before taking off the $60,000 exemption). The estate tax on an estate of that size is about $20,000. $40,000/$160,000ths, or $5,000, of that tax is attributable to the gift, and only that much of the gift tax can be used to reduce the estate tax.

(To be quite accurate, the figure above the line in the above fraction—$40,000—should be reduced by part of the "annual exclusion" that was allowed in figuring the gift tax.)

But very often—especially in large estates, and where the property given away has not fallen in value—the exception

---

HOW TO FIGURE THE GIFT TAX CREDIT IN CASE GIFT WAS

TO WIFE OR HUSBAND

In connection with the credit for gift tax, how much of the estate tax is "attributable to the gift" in a situation where the gift was to the wife or husband?

Clearly, a gift is responsible for none of the estate tax if every dollar of the gift can be used by the estate as a marital deduction (see page 131). In that case there could be no credit for the gift tax paid.

But where the top limit on the marital deduction is exceeded by the total gifts and bequests to the spouse, then only a part of any particular gift is effective in producing a marital deduction; and the balance of that particular gift is responsible for some of the estate tax.

First, therefore, you find this remaining part of the gift that causes estate tax. Then you find what fraction this is of all the property in the estate that causes tax (the gross estate less the marital and charitable deducions). That fraction of the estate tax is the amount attributable to the gift, and is the limit on the gift tax credit.

---

does not come into play and the entire amount of gift tax comes off the estate tax.

AMOUNT OF CREDIT FOR ESTATE TAX ON PRIOR TRANSFERS: To compute this credit, certain limitations are applied to the estate tax paid by the "first" estate. These limitations are intended to produce the true amount of tax that is attributable to the property passing from one estate to the other.

Then the amount as so limited is allowed as a credit to the "second" estate . . .

in full, if the two deaths occurred within a two-year
period;

to the extent of 80%, if the first death occurred within the
3rd or 4th year preceding the second;

to the extent of 60%, if the first death occurred within the
5th or 6th year preceding the second;

to the extent of 40%, if the first death occurred within the
7th or 8th year preceding the second;

to the extent of 20%, if the first death occurred within the
9th or 10th year preceding the second.

After 10 years no credit is allowed.

The computation of this credit for estate tax on prior
transfers is difficult indeed in some situations. However, all
of that arithmetic is the concern of the executor of an estate,
rather than of the person who is just trying to estimate
what the tax will be on his estate. Obviously, you cannot
know that your own estate will ever be entitled to such a
credit. So ignore it.

"Shouldn't I keep inherited property apart from my other
property," you may ask, "so it can be identified?" No. Tracing or identification of the prior taxed property is no longer
necessary. However, if you have inherited some property
within the past 10 years, you had better make sure that the
records of the first estate—copies of tax returns, inventories,
etc.—are available, for they may be needed by your executor.
This is so even in the case of property left by one spouse to
another. (Such property qualifies for the credit to the extent
it did not give the first estate a marital deduction.)

6

Who Is to Bear the Burden of the Tax?

▶ *Tax paid as though it were a debt of the estate.
Tax allocated to the various legatees, etc.
Effect on the marital and charitable deductions.
How to get out of the "squirrel cage."*

Your *executor* will be required to pay the tax on your estate.
But where will he get the money?

You have a choice. You can have the full amount of the tax paid as though it were a debt of the estate; or you can have the tax split up and part of it charged against each person's share of the estate. It all depends on how you word your will.

▶ If you say nothing about the matter one way or the other in your will, the executor will be guided by the law of your State in charging the tax. The Federal tax law also would have a bearing on the question if your estate includes insurance proceeds or property passing under a power of appointment.

PAID AS A DEBT

Mr. Smith, we'll say, is a widower. He says in his will that he wants the Federal estate tax paid as though it were a debt of his estate. His will gives $40,000 to his brother and the rest of his estate—after debts, expenses, and taxes are paid—to his son.

When Mr. Smith dies his estate has a net value of $160,000. That's what remains after all debts, expenses, and so forth have been paid—except the Federal estate tax, which is about $20,000.

So, under the will, the brother gets $40,000, the government gets $20,000, and the son gets $100,000. In effect, all the Federal tax is paid out of the son's share, the so-called "residuary estate."

If insurance, jointly owned property, or other "outside" property is included in the gross estate for tax purposes, the will could provide that the tax on this property too should be paid as a debt and, in effect, charged to the residuary legatee.

CHARGED TO THE VARIOUS SHARES OF THE ESTATE

Assume that Mr. Jones is in exactly the same situation as Mr. Smith—same sized estate and same plan of distribution between brother and son—except that Mr. Jones provides in his will that each person's share of the estate shall bear a proportionate part of the Federal tax.

The brother's $40,000 share is one-fourth of the $160,000 that's on hand. Therefore, the brother's share will be reduced by $5,000—one-fourth of the tax—and the brother will receive $35,000.

The son's residuary share will be reduced by $15,000— three-fourths of the tax—and he will receive $105,000.

Under Jones's plan, the residuary legatee doesn't pay more than his fair share of the tax.

MARITAL AND CHARITABLE DEDUCTIONS MAY BE AFFECTED

The choice between these two ways of having the tax paid is not essentially a tax matter. When you choose a method, you determine how your property will be divided among your beneficiaries. You would not expect your choice to have any bearing on the total amount of the tax.

However, there are situations where the method does affect the total amount of Federal tax. Generally speaking, such a situation exists whenever property is left under a will to a surviving wife or husband or to a "charity."

That is because the marital and charitable deductions are measured by the actual amount of property passing to the spouse or to the charity. If you arrange matters so that some or all of the tax will come out of your spouse's share of the estate or out of a share going to a charity, then your marital or charitable deduction will be just that much less.

TAKE ANOTHER LOOK AT YOUR TAX

In applying these facts to your own situation, you may find that you are not quite through with the estimate of the tax on your estate.

In the preceding chapter you have calculated your tax. Very well, how will the tax be paid? Will some of it come out of the residuary estate that you are leaving to your wife or husband? Will some of it go to reduce a bequest to a charity?

If you determine that one of these deductible shares of your estate is affected by the tax, better go back and make a rough estimate of the "damage." The problem isn't easy. The amount of the deduction depends on the amount of the tax, and the tax depends on the deduction. It's a regular squirrel cage. If you are good at algebra, you can get out of it—re-estimate your deduction exactly. (See how to do it, page 286.) But for your present purposes, an adjustment in round figures to the deduction may be quite satisfactory.

Part Three

THE FEDERAL GIFT TAX IN OUTLINE

7

A Quick Look at Gift Tax

> ► *What is the gift tax, who pays it, and why is there such a tax? Small gifts. The $3,000 annual exclusions. "Future interests." The $30,000 "lifetime exemption." Who must file a return?*

WHAT IS THE FEDERAL GIFT TAX?

It is a tax on gifts made by individuals.

WHO PAYS THE TAX—THE PERSON WHO MAKES THE GIFT?

Yes, the donor is primarily responsible for paying it and does pay it in nearly all cases. But if it isn't paid when due, the government can collect from the donee.

WHY SHOULD A PERSON BE TAXED FOR GIVING AWAY HIS MONEY?

If there were no gift tax the government would have a hard time collecting *estate* tax. People would give away all their property before they died. They would give it to their children, grandchildren, or other members of their families —to the persons who someday would get their property anyway.

THE GIFT TAX DOESN'T PUT A STOP TO THESE GIFTS DURING LIFE, DOES IT?

No, it just puts a tax on them. In fact, there is still a tax advantage in making gifts. Generally, it's cheaper to pay gift tax than estate tax.

See Chapter 15 on this point. The tax on gifts by married persons may be especially low on account of the privilege to "split" gifts between a husband and wife.

IS GIFT TAX MEASURED BY THE MARKET VALUE OF THE PROPERTY GIVEN AWAY?

Yes, by its market value at date of the gift. The cost of the property is immaterial, so far as the gift tax is concerned.

ARE SMALL GIFTS TAXED? WHAT ABOUT CHRISTMAS PRESENTS, BIRTHDAY PRESENTS, WEDDING GIFTS?

It wouldn't be practical to tax small, everyday gifts, so there's a $3,000 annual exemption (or "exclusion," as it is technically called). Here is the general rule: The first $3,000 of gifts you make to any person in any year is not counted as a gift.

EXAMPLE: *In 1955 Mr. Smith makes several gifts to his daughter totaling $2,800. Result: the gifts are wiped out by the exclusion. Mr. Smith does not even have to report them on a gift tax return.*

In 1955 Mr. Smith also makes gifts to his son totaling $3,500. Result: Mr. Smith must report the $3,500 on a gift tax return (due on or before April 15, 1956). On the return he takes off the $3,000 exclusion, leaving only $500 of gifts.

In 1955 Mr. Smith also gives $5,000 to each of five grandchildren. Result: the $25,000 is reported on the return and reduced by $15,000 of exclusions, leaving $10,000 of gifts.

*Thus, Mr. Smith's 1955 gift tax return shows a
total of $10,500 gifts over and above the exclusion.
For the sake of clarity, let's call this $10,500 the
total of Mr. Smith's "clear" gifts.*

CAN YOU GET MORE THAN ONE $3,000 EXCLUSION?

Yes. You have a $3,000 exclusion for each donee. You
could give hundreds of thousands of dollars away, free of
tax, if you divided it among enough persons. And you
could do the same thing the following year, and the year
after that.

ARE THERE ANY EXCEPTIONS TO THIS GENERAL RULE?

There is one exception. If you give anybody a "future
interest" in property, there is no $3,000 exclusion for the
gift; it is all taxable.

Briefly, a future interest is a right to use property only
in the future. The United States Supreme Court says it is
any property interest, "whether vested or contingent, limited
to commence in use, possession or enjoyment at some future
date or time."

The commonest example is the remainder of a trust. The
income beneficiary usually has a "present interest" in the
trust property, the remaindermen have "future interests."
But if the income of the trust is to be accumulated, everyone's interest is "future" (except in certain cases where income is accumulated for a minor—See Tax-Saving Idea
No. 8, at p. 35).

IF YOU GIVE SOMEONE A $1,000 BOND THAT MATURES TWENTY YEARS FROM NOW, IS THAT A FUTURE INTEREST?

No. The mere fact that a bond, note, or insurance policy

is payable in the future doesn't make the ownership of it a future interest.

SUPPOSE, LIKE MR. SMITH, YOU MAKE "CLEAR" GIFTS OF $500 AND $10,000 IN 1955, OR A TOTAL OF $10,500. ABOUT HOW MUCH WOULD YOUR TAX BE?

You might not have to pay any tax at all for 1955. That is because you may be entitled to reduce the total amount of your "clear" gifts by certain deductions before arriving at your net, or "taxable," gifts. The tax rates are applied against the net figure.

WHAT ARE THESE GIFT TAX DEDUCTIONS?

There are three:
1. The charitable deduction (for gifts to charities, etc.),
2. The marital deduction (for half the value of gifts to wife or husband), and
3. The "lifetime exemption."

HOW MUCH IS THIS "LIFETIME EXEMPTION"?

It is $30,000. But you can't deduct that much each year. Under present law you can deduct only $30,000 in your whole lifetime. Most people use the exemption as soon as they need it, applying it against their earliest gifts.

EXAMPLE: *The only sizable gifts Mr. Jones has ever made (since the start of the present gift tax system in 1932) are $10,000 to his daughter in 1945 and $40,000 to his son in 1955.*

In 1945 his "clear" gift was $7,000, after taking off the $3,000 annual exclusion. On his gift tax

*return for that year he used $7,000 of his lifetime
exemption to wipe out the gift, leaving $23,000
of the exemption for use in later years.*

*In 1955 he takes the annual exclusion off the
$40,000 gift, reducing it to $37,000. He uses the
remaining $23,000 lifetime exemption to bring
the net taxable gift down to $14,000. He pays a
tax on the $14,000.*

THEN A PERSON WHO HASN'T MADE "CLEAR" GIFTS IN THE PAST
CAN NOW GIVE SOMEBODY $33,000 WITHOUT PAYING A TAX?

Yes. The $3,000 annual exclusion would reduce the gift
to $30,000 (unless it's a future interest). The lifetime ex-
emption would reduce it to zero.

You can do even better than that if you are married. See
"Gifts to Your Wife or Husband" (Chapter 10) and "Split
Gifts" (Chapter 11). And in the case of gifts to charities,
etc., there's no limit on the amounts. See "The Charitable
Deduction" (Chapter 9).

DO ANY OF THE STATES OR TERRITORIES HAVE GIFT TAXES?

Twelve of them do: California, Colorado, Louisiana, Min-
nesota, North Carolina, Oklahoma, Oregon, Rhode Island,
Tennessee, Virginia, Washington and Wisconsin. These
taxes are low compared to the Federal tax. They are not
deductible in figuring the Federal tax and cannot be used
in any way as a credit against the Federal tax.

IS THE FEDERAL GIFT TAX DEDUCTIBLE IN FIGURING THE FEDERAL
INCOME TAX?

No.

IS THE PERSON WHO RECEIVES A GIFT REQUIRED
TO REPORT IT?

Yes, he must file a "donee's gift tax return" showing
gifts in excess of the $3,000 exclusion, or gifts of future
interests in any amount.

If the gift is in trust, the trustee usually takes care
of filing this return.

IS THE GIFT TAX JUST A PART OF THE INCOME TAX?

No it is a separate tax. People are confused about this
sometimes because the gift tax is payable annually and the
return is due the same date that most income tax returns
are due (April 15, for gifts made in 1955 and later).

WHAT ARE THE REQUIREMENTS FOR FILING A GIFT TAX RETURN?

You must file a return for any year in which you have
made gifts in excess of the $3,000 exclusion, or gifts of
future interests in any amount.

If you consent to have a gift by your husband or wife
taxed as though it had been made half by you (see "Split
Gifts," Chapter 11), you are considered the donor of your
share. Thus, even though you make no gifts but your husband or wife does, you may be required to file a return.

*Before you decide you don't need to file a return, read
Chapter 8, "What Are Gifts?" You may have made gifts
without knowing it.*

CAN A HUSBAND AND WIFE FILE A JOINT RETURN?

There is no such thing as a joint return for gift tax. Each
person files his own return.

8

What Are Gifts?

► *U. S. Savings Bonds. Joint bank accounts. Life insurance. "Tax-exempt" securities. Sales for less than value. Loans not expected to be repaid. Cancellation of debts. Support of family. Partnership interests. Gifts to corporations. Gifts by minors. Premarital and divorce settlements. Powers of appointment. Trusts.*

The gift tax Regulations say:

All transactions whereby property or property rights or interests are gratuitously passed or conferred upon another, regardless of the means or device employed, constitute gifts subject to tax.

Most of us think we know a gift when we see one. But the fact is that the gift tax applies to many transactions that may not at first appear to be gifts.

On the other hand, certain other transactions may appear to be gifts but aren't.

Here is a check list to help you decide if you have made any gifts in the past and to help you know if your plans ahead involve any gifts:

U. S. SAVINGS BONDS

Suppose you use your own money to buy U. S. Savings Bonds and have them put in your name, payable on death to someone else. You are *not* making a gift.

THESE ARE NOT GIFTS

Mr. and Mrs. Jones file a joint Federal income tax return for 1954. He pays the tax with his own money, although a good deal of the income shown on the return was hers.

Mrs. Jones gave a large sum of money to her son in 1954. Under the "split-gifts" provision of the gift tax law, Mr. Jones consents to have the gift taxed half to himself. He pays the gift tax with his own money.

The gift tax Regulations make it clear that, in paying these taxes, Mr. Jones makes no gift to his wife.

If you gratuitously have the bonds put in the sole name of someone else, you are making a gift to that person in amount of the cost of the bonds. The same is true if you have the bonds registered in that person's name, payable on death to a third person.

You may decide to register bonds in the names of two other persons as co-owners—such as "Mary Jones or Helen Jones." You are making a gift to each in amount of half the cost of the bonds.

Now for the most important point:

If you put the bonds in your name and somebody else's as co-owners—such as "John Jones [you] or Mary Jones"—then you make no gift unless and until you permit the co-owner to cash the bonds while you are living and keep the proceeds. If you do permit that, you are making a gift in amount of the proceeds.

JOINT BANK ACCOUNTS

If you open a bank account for yourself and someone else, and if you have the right to take out all the money without the other person's consent, you make no gift unless and until the other person withdraws some of the money for his or her own benefit.

What if there is such a withdrawal? The amount of the gift is the amount withdrawn.

▶ Notice that there is no gift unless the money withdrawn is *for the benefit* of the other person. If a man's wife takes money out of a joint checking account to pay household bills or necessary clothing expenses, there is no gift by the husband. The money is really used for *his* benefit, inasmuch as he is legally obligated to pay such expenses.

OTHER JOINTLY HELD PROPERTY

"JOINT TENANTS": If you use your own money to buy a house, an automobile, a stock or bond, or almost any other item of property, and then have the asset put in the names of yourself and someone else as "joint tenants with right of survivorship," you are making a gift to the other person, your co-owner.

The amount of the gift is half the value of the property. The "value of the property" means the equity—the full value less any mortgage.

EXAMPLE: *A man buys a house for $20,000 giving $15,000 cash and a $5,000 mortgage. He puts the property in his and his son's name as joint tenants. Tax Result: He has made a gift to his son of $7,500. If the father later pays off $1,000 of the mortgage, he is giving his son $500. Or if he spends $1,000 improving the property (not just repairing it or maintaining it), he also makes a $500 gift to the son.*

TWO TAXES ON JOINTLY HELD PROPERTY—HOW THE GIFT TAX CREDIT HELPS

If you make a gift by sharing the ownership of your property with somebody else, the entire property may still be treated for estate tax purposes as though it were a part of your estate.

That means there could be an estate tax on the property even though you may already have paid a gift tax on it.

There isn't necessarily a double tax burden on the taxpayer, though. Your estate would be entitled to a "gift tax credit"—the amount being limited to the estate tax that is attributable to the gift. For an explanation of this credit, see Chapter 5.

► But in the case of real estate owned jointly by a husband and wife, the donor (the one who furnishes most of the consideration) need not report such transactions after 1954 as gifts for gift tax purposes. See "Tax Relief under the 1954 Tax Law," following at p. 161.

"TENANTS BY THE ENTIRETY": Now let's alter the preceding situation slightly. Say the purchaser, a married man, has the property put in his and his wife's names as "tenants by the entirety." Under the law of their state, neither of them, acting alone, "can defeat the right of the survivor to the whole of the property."

Those are technical words. If you and your wife or husband own property jointly, better ask your lawyer if you are "tenants by the entirety." You may well be. It is one of the most popular ways of owning the family home in some States.

The husband, in these circumstances, would be making a gift to his wife. Would the amount of the gift be half the value of the property? Not necessarily. If she is younger than he, then her interest in the property is generally considered to be worth more than his. If she is older than he, then her interest is worth less.

The Commissioner of Internal Revenue will help compute the value of the gift in a case of this nature. But for a rule of thumb, remember this: If the ages of husband and wife are *approximately* equal, then the amount of the gift is *approximately* half the value of the property.

▶ But in the case of real estate owned jointly by a husband and wife, the donor (the one who furnishes most of the consideration) need not report such transactions after 1954 as gifts for gift tax purposes. See "Tax Relief under the 1954 Tax Law," below.

Tax relief under the 1954 tax law: The 1954 tax law —the "Internal Revenue Code of 1954"—eliminated a troublesome tax trap that many married couples have been falling into. It provided that, after 1954, no gift shall be considered to take place at the creation of a tenancy in common in real estate, or a tenancy by the entirety in real estate—or when a mortgage payment occurs, or when improvements are made—unless the spouse who furnishes most of the money elects otherwise.

If he does nothing—if he simply omits the filing of a gift tax return, for example—no gift tax liability then arises. Later, if the two owners should decide to split or "break up" the joint ownership arrangement, a gift would be considered to occur if the division of the property or the proceeds is disproportionate to the way they originally paid for it. But if the property is kept jointly owned until one of the spouses dies, there is never a gift tax.

It may or may not be advisable for a married person to take advantage of this new relief provision. (See "What to Do about Jointly Owned Real Estate under the 1954 Tax Law," at p. 73.) Moreover, it should be kept in mind that the new provision applies only to real estate held by husbands and wives as joint tenants with right of survivorship or as tenants by the entirety: it does *not* apply to real estate held jointly by other owners, nor does it apply to securities or other personal property, even if held by husbands and wives.

One last point: the action taken by a married person with respect to *gift* tax on jointly owned property has no effect on the inclusion of the property in his estate for *estate* tax purposes when he dies. The full value of the property would be included in his gross estate if he paid all the purchase price; and this would be so even though he reported a gift when he put the property in his and his wife's joint names. Some or all of the gift tax paid, however, could be used as a credit against the estate tax.

SPLITTING UP JOINTLY OWNED PROPERTY: Suppose you want to take property out of joint names. Do you run into a gift tax?

The general rules are as follows:

> No gift occurs if the property has been held by both of you as "joint tenants with right of survivorship" and you divide it equally (by putting it in your names as tenants in common, for instance). If you divide it unequally there would be a gift *by* the one who gets the smaller share *to* the one who gets the larger share.

"TENANTS IN COMMON"

A tenant in common owns a stated share of the property, a share that he can sell, give away, or bequeath in his will. If he gives it away, the gift is taxed. There are no special gift tax problems connected with this form of ownership, and we do not mean to include it when we talk here about "jointly owned property."

Examples of Tenancy in Common: Real estate is sometimes held this way. Upon the death of one owner, the surviving owners are none the richer. A partnership interest might be said to be a special form of tenancy in common. So is community property, in a sense.

If the property has been held by a husband and wife as "tenants by the entirety," a government ruling says the same principles apply as when that form of ownership is created. In other words, an equal division would not represent a large gift by either the husband or the wife if they were about the same age.

An exception to these general rules comes into play if, after 1954, a husband or wife took advantage of the relief provision in the 1954 tax law and did not report a gift when real estate was put in the joint names of the couple.

LIFE INSURANCE TRANSACTIONS

You may gratuitously assign one of your insurance policies—so that you no longer can borrow on it, surrender it for cash, change the beneficiary, and so forth. If your own estate is not the beneficiary, then you are making a gift.

► The amount of the gift is the price an insurance company would charge for a similar contract, if that figure is obtainable. Otherwise the amount of the gift is the policy "reserve" at the date of the gift, with an adjustment for premiums paid ahead.

If you pay a premium on a policy that belongs to someone else, you are making a gift. The amount of the gift is the amount of the premium.

Suppose you merely change the beneficiary of one of your policies. You are not making a gift so long as you have the right to make further changes. What if you irrevocably name a beneficiary? There would be no gift if you still had the right to borrow on the policy or surrender it for cash.

"TAX-EXEMPT" SECURITIES

State and municipal bonds are tax exempt in the sense that interest paid on them is exempt from Federal income tax. But there is no gift tax exemption. All bonds—even those issued by the Federal government, the States, territories, and by cities, counties, and towns—are subject to Federal gift tax if given away.

SALES AND EXCHANGES FOR LESS THAN TRUE VALUE

Suppose you own an asset that's clearly worth $1,000. You sell this for $600 to your brother-in-law or some other relative or member of your family. You make a gift of $400.

The same would be true if, in a nonbusiness deal of some kind, you *exchanged* an asset worth $1,000 for something worth much less. If you give somebody a bargain, you're probably making a gift.

But the gift tax Regulations say that these general principles do not apply to ordinary business transactions. If a business transaction is "bona fide, at arm's length, and free from donative intent," the price or other consideration given for an asset will be regarded as adequate and the parties will not face a gift tax.

"LOANS" NOT EXPECTED TO BE REPAID

It has been held that "loans" made with no expectation they would be repaid were, in fact, gifts rather than loans. The gifts were considered made when the loans were granted.

CANCELLATION OF DEBTS

The cancellation of a debt *may* constitute a gift.

Suppose the borrower is able to repay. The lender, with the intention of helping out the borrower, tells him the debt is forgiven. The lender is making a gift.

But the lender is not making a gift when he writes off a debt that is, in fact, uncollectible. Neither does he make a gift if he is compensated in some way for canceling the debt.

Here is a rough rule: *If you cancel a debt for personal reasons, you probably are making a gift. If you cancel a debt for purely business reasons, you probably are not making a gift.*

PAYMENTS FOR SUPPORT AND MAINTENANCE OF WIFE AND MINOR CHILDREN

Generally a man is legally obligated to support his wife and minor children. Therefore he is making no gifts to them when he provides for their usual and accustomed support (including education, in the case of the children).

BRINGING WIFE, CHILDREN, OR OTHER RELATIVES INTO A BUSINESS AS PARTNERS

A businessman who gives his wife, child, or relative a share in his unincorporated business may incur a gift tax.

That is so, at least, if the new partner is going to be inactive in the business. In a situation where a man brought his two sons in as partners, it was ruled that he made no gifts to them inasmuch as they were expected to gradually take over the active management of the business; they contributed their services in return for their father's contribution of capital.

Each case of this nature depends on the particular facts and circumstances. The only safe rule: Ask your lawyer about the gift tax consequences before you part with a share of your business.

"GIFTS" TO A CORPORATION

A voluntary payment by a stockholder to a closely held company is usually made in return for some valuable benefit passing to the stockholder, and therefore it is not likely to be a gift.

If it actually should be considered a gift, is it a gift to the other stockholders? Should the amount of the gift be reduced on account of the interest in the company held by the donor? These questions are not well settled. It does appear, however, that a person who owns 100 per cent of a company's stock does not make a gift by transferring money or property to his company (if the company is solvent); he would be benefiting nobody but himself.

"GIFTS" BY A MINOR

A person under age can hardly make a valid, irrevocable gift. Where a minor does attempt to give property away, it has been held that a gift for purposes of the gift tax occurs at the time the minor later becomes of age and does not disaffirm the gift.

PREMARITAL SETTLEMENTS

Under State law, a wife usually is entitled to a certain minimum part of her husband's estate when he dies, regardless of what his will says. A husband, too, may be entitled to a minimum share of his wife's estate.

Before a wealthy person marries, therefore, he sometimes strikes a bargain with his intended spouse. He immediately gives her a certain amount of property and she agrees, in return, not to claim her minimum share of his estate.

Is the amount he gives her a gift?

The U. S. Supreme Court has held that it is.

PAYMENTS CONNECTED WITH DIVORCES AND LEGAL SEPARATIONS

In connection with a divorce or legal separation, one of the parties often pays a large sum in settlement of property and support rights. Is it a gift?

The 1954 tax law (effective, as to gift tax, after 1954) provides that transfers of property by husband and wife pursuant to a written agreement relative to their marital and property rights or to support minor children will be free of gift tax if divorce occurs within two years after the agreement. This is so whether or not the agreement is approved by the divorce decree.

POWERS OF APPOINTMENT

You may be a beneficiary under a trust made by someone else. Do you have the right to name the persons to receive the principal after your death? Do you have the right to withdraw any of the principal during your life?

If you have any such right, and if it's a broad, unrestricted right (a "general" power of appointment, that is), it may cause the entire trust fund to be included in your estate for Federal estate tax. This is so, in some cases, whether you actually exercise the power or not; mere possession of it may be an estate tax liability. (See, on this point, page 120.)

One way to escape the estate tax might be to give up the power, if that is possible and feasible. In doing so, would you be making a gift subject to the Federal gift tax?

The gift tax law says the release of a "general" power of appointment will not be taxed as a gift if the power was created on or before October 21, 1942. If the power was created after that date, a release now would constitute a gift and, possibly, would result in gift tax liability.

For full details on the treatment of powers of appointment under the Federal gift tax, see section 2514 of the Internal Revenue Act of 1954.

TRUSTS

Assume that Mr. Smith puts aside $100,000 in a "living trust"—a trust that becomes effective while he is living. In the trust agreement he says (in the proper legal language, of course):

I want the income paid to my daughter so long as she lives. When she dies, the trust is to end and the principal is to be divided among any children of hers who are then living. If there aren't any such children, pay the money to my brother or his estate. I am not keeping any control over this trust; it is irrevocable.

In establishing this trust, Mr. Smith is making gifts:
(a) to the daughter, and
(b) to her children or his brother.

The total value of the gifts is $100,000, the amount put in the trust.

The amount of the gift to the daughter depends on her age when the money is deposited in the trust. She gets the income for life. The younger she is—and the greater her life expectancy—the more this "life estate" is worth to her. A table in the gift tax Regulations makes it easy to figure the amount of her gift, once you know her age and the amount put in the trust. (The table is given on page 270.)

The amount of the gift to the daughter's children or to the brother is $100,000 less the daughter's gift. It can't be known just who will receive this gift; but, in figuring Mr. Smith's gift tax, it doesn't matter. It's a gift of a future interest, and whether it goes to one person or is divided among several, there's no $3,000 annual exclusion allowed for it.

There will be a $3,000 annual exclusion allowed against the gift to the daughter. Her life estate is a "present interest"; it begins immediately.

Now let's vary the terms of this trust and see how it affects Mr. Smith's gift tax:

REVOCABLE TRUST: Suppose, instead of making the trust irrevocable, Mr. Smith had kept the right to change the trust in any way or to take the property back. RESULT: There would have been no gift to anyone. Revocable gifts aren't taxed. They aren't considered to be complete and final.

ANNUAL INCOME: This revocable trust would pay income to the daughter. Would the income payments be considered gifts each year as they were made? Yes. They would be gifts by Mr. Smith to his daughter. They would be gifts of present interests, with a $3,000 exclusion allowed each year.

POWER TO CHANGE BENEFICIARY: Suppose Mr. Smith could not take the property back but did keep the right to name someone other than his daughter to be beneficiary of the income. RESULT: The gifts would still be incomplete and Mr. Smith would have no gift tax to pay. The right on his part to make even a slight change in the distribution of the income could operate to keep the gifts tentative and incomplete.

REVOCABLE WITH CONSENT OF BENEFICIARY: Suppose Mr. Smith could revoke the trust and take the property back, but only if his daughter consented. RESULT: The gifts would be complete. The daughter would suffer a substantial loss if the trust should be canceled; under those circumstances the trust is, for all practical purposes, irrevocable.

REVOCABLE WITH CONSENT OF TRUSTEE: What if Mr. Smith could revoke the trust provided he got the trustee's consent to do so. RESULT: The trust would be considered revocable and there would be no gifts. The trustee might have no reason to withhold consent. It's almost as though Mr. Smith, acting alone, could revoke.

POSSIBILITY THAT PROPERTY WILL COME BACK: Suppose Mr. Smith had kept no control over the trust. But he provided that, if he should be living when the daughter dies, the property should come back to him—instead of being given to the daughter's children or to his brother. RESULT: There would be a gift of the life estate to the daughter. There would also be a gift to her children or to Mr. Smith's brother. But the amount of that gift can be reduced by a value allotted to Mr. Smith's chances of getting back the property. An actuary could make such a valuation without any difficulty.

LIFE ESTATE NOT GIVEN AWAY: Suppose Mr. Smith, instead of giving the income to his daughter for her life, had made himself the beneficiary for his life. RESULT: The only gifts would be to the persons benefiting from the property after Mr. Smith's death. The amount of those gifts would be $100,000 less the value of Mr. Smith's life estate.

TRUST FOR A CHILD: Suppose the trust is irrevocable and is for the daughter, just as in the situation we started with. But assume the daughter is a minor at the time Mr. Smith establishes the trust. So Mr. Smith provides in the trust agreement that the income shall be accumulated for her until she is 21. RESULT: *All* the gifts are future interests. There is no $3,000 annual exclusion, even as to the daughter's life estate. She won't possess or enjoy that life estate until she becomes twenty-one.

If Mr. Smith should provide in the trust agreement that the trust should end when the daughter becomes 21, with all the income and principal going to her at that time, and if certain other provisions were made with respect to the income and principal while the daughter is a minor, a $3,000 exclusion would be available. See, on this type of trust, Tax-Saving Idea No. 8, at page 35. This quite limited bit of tax relief was allowed by the 1954 tax law, effective as to gift tax in 1955 and later years. As a general rule, it can still be said that most practical kinds of accumulation trusts are gifts of future interests—not present interests.

REMAINDER TO A CHARITY: Suppose Mr. Smith's trust provided for income to the daughter for life, with principal payable at her death to a charitable organization. RESULT: There would be gifts to the daughter and to the charity, if the trust is irrevocable. But only the gift to the daughter would be taxed; charitable gifts are tax free.

DOUBTFUL GIFTS TO CHARITY: In the preceding situation, what if the trustee was authorized by the trust agreement to pay the daughter some of the principal, in addition to the income, if she should need the extra money in an emergency? RESULT: It might be impossible to say how much, if anything, the charity would ever receive. In that case the whole fund might be considered a gift to the daughter and taxed in full.

These are only a few of the many types of living trusts. If you have established a trust for members of your family, or if you plan to establish one, ask your attorney how it affects or how it will affect your gift tax.

9

The Deductions Are Few
but Important

▶ *The charitable deduction. The marital deduction. The $30,000 "lifetime exemption."*

After you have figured out the gifts you have made in a
certain year and after you have taken off the $3,000 annual
exclusions (except for gifts of future interests), you are
entitled to take off your DEDUCTIONS.

There are only three gift tax deductions:

    (1) the charitable deduction (for gifts to charities, etc.);
    (2) the marital deduction (for half the value of gifts
        to wife or husband);
    (3) the "lifetime exemption."

THE CHARITABLE DEDUCTION

The word "charitable" covers a lot of ground. The gift
tax law says that, in computing your taxable gifts for a
calendar year, you can deduct:

    ... the amount of such gifts to or for the use of:

        (1) the United States, any State, Territory, or any political
            subdivision thereof, or the District of Columbia,
            —for exclusively public purposes;

173

(2) a corporation, or trust, or community chest, fund, or foundation, organized and operated exclusively for religious, charitable, scientific, literary, or educational purposes, including the encouragement of art and the prevention of cruelty to children or animals.

—provided no part of the net earnings of such organization inures to the benefit of any private shareholder or individual, and no substantial part of its activities is carrying on propaganda, or otherwise attempting to influence legislation;

(3) a fraternal society, order, or association, operating under the lodge system,

—provided such gifts are to be used by such fraternal society, order, or association exclusively for one or more of the purposes enumerated in (2);

(4) any organization of war veterans or auxiliary unit or society thereof,

—if such organization, auxiliary unit, or society thereof is organized in the United States or any of its possessions, and if no part of its net earnings inures to the benefit of any private shareholder or individual.

No LIMIT: Notice that you can deduct the amount of *all* charitable gifts. There is no limit, such as there is on the "contributions" deduction on a Federal income tax return.

You CAN CREATE YOUR OWN CHARITY: Under paragraph 2, there is no requirement that the gift be to an already-existing trust. You can create your own charitable trust by means of a living trust agreement, if you wish. The trust would have to be irrevocable, of course. (But see "Watch Out for 'Prohibited Transactions,'" page 126.)

"PROHIBITED TRANSACTIONS" WILL ENDANGER
GIFT TAX DEDUCTIONS

You can put money aside in a trust for yourself and also for
a charity—as Mr. Smith does in the example on this page—
and pay no gift tax, *provided the trust does not engage in
"prohibited transactions."*

See "Watch Out for 'Prohibited Transactions,' " page 126.
The payment of income to Mr. Smith himself is not a prohibited transaction since that income is not claimed to be
held for or set aside for the charity.

You can combine personal and charitable gifts: Under
(2) it is stated that a trust must be "organized and operated
exclusively" for charitable, etc., purposes. But that doesn't
mean that you or members of your family can't receive income from the trust for a while.

EXAMPLE: *Mr. Smith establishes an irrevocable living trust.
The trust agreement instructs the trustee to pay
all the income to Mr. Smith himself while he
lives. At his death the principal is to be paid to
(or held for the sole benefit of) a certain charity.*

In establishing this trust, Mr. Smith would be giving to
the charity a part of every dollar he puts in it. The rest of
the dollar would represent the cost of his own "life estate."
Thus, he makes only one gift—to the charity—and that's
deductible. So he pays no gift tax.

► He would also be entitled to a contributions deduction
on his Federal income tax return (up to the 20% or 30%

limit) for this same gift to the charity. The trust would cost him no gift tax; and it would save income tax for him.

CHARITABLE GIFTS ARE NOT TAXED, BUT YOU MUST REPORT THEM: If you give $10,000 to a charity, it can never add to your gift tax. Nevertheless, you would have to report the gift on a gift tax return, since it is more than $3,000. (Or it might be a future interest. Gifts of future interests, regardless of amount, must be reported.)

On the gift tax return you would report the full $10,000; then take off the $3,000 annual exclusion (if it's a gift of a present interest), leaving $7,000. Then you'd take a charitable deduction of $7,000, leaving nothing to be taxed.

THE MARITAL DEDUCTION

Husbands and wives are now taxed for only half the value of gifts passing between them.

EXAMPLE: *Mr. Smith gives Mrs. Smith $10,000 in 1955. (This is a real gift, over and above the amount she needs for household expenses, clothing, and other necessities.)*

The $3,000 annual exclusion reduces the gift to $7,000, and a $5,000 "marital deduction" (half of $10,000) reduces it to $2,000.

This marital deduction for gift tax is discussed at length in the following chapter.

THE "LIFETIME EXEMPTION"

Every United States citizen or resident can deduct a $30,000 lifetime exemption.

You can't deduct that much each year. You can deduct only $30,000 in your whole lifetime.

This deduction was $40,000 a few years back, and before that it was $50,000. Some persons, therefore, have made large gifts in past years and have already used more than $30,000. The way this situation is handled is discussed in Chapter 12, "How to Figure Your Tax."

10

Gifts to Your Wife or Husband Are Only Half Taxed

▶ *What is the marital deduction for gift tax? How does it save gift tax? What kind of gifts qualify for the deduction?*

Two new features were added to the gift tax law by the Revenue Act of 1948. One was the marital deduction, discussed in this chapter. The other was the provision for "split gifts," covered in the next chapter.

WHAT IS THE MARITAL DEDUCTION?

The marital deduction is allowed for half the value of gifts made by a husband to his wife or by a wife to her husband.

For example, if a man gives his wife $8,000 during a certain year, he is entitled to a marital deduction of $4,000 in figuring his gift tax. The deduction cuts the gift in half.

The marital deduction is in addition to the $3,000 annual exclusion. In the case of the husband's $8,000 gift, for example, he would take off $3,000 (the annual exclusion) and $4,000 (the marital deduction), leaving only $1,000 to be taxed. He could even wipe out the $1,000 by using $1,000 of his $30,000 lifetime exemption, if he hasn't used it all up already.

178

HOW TO GIVE $150,000 TO YOUR WIFE
WITHOUT PAYING A GIFT TAX

A man might be able to give his wife considerably more than $6,000 a year and still escape the tax. He could use his lifetime exemption to wipe out the gifts.

EXAMPLE:

Gifts to wife in 1955	$10,000
Less the annual exclusion	3,000
	$ 7,000
Less the marital deduction (½ of $10,000)	5,000
	$ 2,000
Less $2,000 of the $30,000 lifetime exemption	2,000
	–0–

The husband could continue the $10,000-per-year gifts for fifteen years before he used up all his $30,000 lifetime exemption (provided, of course, the exemption was intact at the start and he didn't thereafter make taxable gifts to other persons).

Thus, he could give her $150,000 without paying a cent of gift tax.

IT ALLOWS $6,000-PER-YEAR GIFTS, FREE OF TAX

"As I see it," a husband may say, "I can now give my wife up to $6,000 every year without ever paying a gift tax."

He is right. The $6,000 gift in each year would be reduced by a $3,000 annual exclusion and a $3,000 marital deduction. He could keep that up indefinitely, without even touching his $30,000 lifetime exemption.

He would, however, be required to file gift tax returns.

A return is still required where a gift in excess of $3,000 has been made to anyone in a year.

IS IT LIKE THE MARITAL DEDUCTION FOR ESTATE TAX?

There is also a marital deduction allowed in figuring the Federal *estate* tax. The gift tax marital deduction is somewhat like the estate tax deduction. But it isn't the same thing, of course, inasmuch as it is allowed for a different tax.

One important difference between the two deductions is in their amounts. Suppose a man leaves his wife $10,000 under his will. His estate is entitled to an estate tax marital deduction for the full $10,000 (unless that, plus the value of property left to his wife in other ways, is more than half his adjusted gross estate). But if he gives his wife $10,000 while he is living, his gift tax marital deduction can't be more than half the gift, or $5,000.

HOW TO MAKE THE GIFTS

With respect to HOW the property must be given to the wife or husband in order to qualify for the deduction, the gift tax rules are modeled after the estate tax rules.

For example, if you give $10,000 to your wife or husband outright, with no strings attached, you will be entitled to the deduction.

But if you try to tie up the money so that your wife or husband doesn't have the full benefit of it, you may possibly lose the deduction.

The following table shows the more common ways you can give property to your wife or husband. "Yes" means you will get the deduction for half the value of the gift. "No" means you won't get a deduction.

METHOD	DEDUCTION?
Outright gift	Yes
By establishing a living trust, spouse has all the income for life and has the unrestricted right to name the persons to receive the principal afterward 　　(In a trust like this it wouldn't matter if the trustee had the right to pay principal to the spouse in emergencies. But the trustee must not have the right to pay principal or income to anybody else.)	Yes
By establishing a living trust, spouse has all the income for life but has no rights in connection with the principal	No
By your buying a house or any other property (except U. S. Savings Bonds) and putting it in names of yourself and spouse as joint tenants or as tenants by the entirety (and, in the case of real estate, you elect to report the transaction as a gift)	Yes (but the gift is only half, or approximately half, the value of the property; so the marital deduction would be about 25 per cent of the value)
By your buying U. S. Savings Bonds, putting them in names of yourself and spouse as co-owners, and then letting your spouse cash the bonds and keep the proceeds	Yes
By letting your spouse withdraw and keep money that you have put in a joint bank account	Yes

METHOD	DEDUCTION?
By buying an annuity for sole benefit of your spouse, with any amounts that may be payable after spouse's death going into her or his estate	Yes
By buying a joint-and-survivor annuity for benefit of yourself and your spouse	No
By changing community property into your spouse's separate property	No

11

Split Gifts

► *Splitting a gift; example. How much tax does splitting save? The rules for splitting.*

A husband and wife can't file a joint gift tax return. There is no such thing as a joint return.

But a husband and wife can do something very much like filing a joint return. They can treat the gifts they make to other persons as though each gave half.

For instance, Mr. Jones gives $10,000 to his daughter in 1955. Mrs. Jones makes no gifts. When it comes time to file gift tax returns (on or before April 15, 1956), Mr. and Mrs. Jones can each file a return reporting a $5,000 gift to the daughter.

Each of them could take off a $3,000 annual exclusion, leaving $2,000. Then each of them could wipe out the $2,000 by using some of his or her $30,000 lifetime exemption.

NO TAX ON A GIFT OF $66,000

In this way a married man might give away as much as $66,000 to one person in a single year without paying a tax. He would report a $33,000 gift, and so would his wife. He would take off the annual exclusion, reducing the gift to $30,000, and so would his wife. Then each of them could use his or her $30,000 lifetime exemption (if none of it has been used so far) to wipe out the gift.

SAVING $13,000 TAX ON A $200,000 GIFT

Splitting gifts in this way is a big help to a married couple if one of them owns the bulk of the family property. In effect, it doubles the gift tax exemptions; and when gifts do exceed these doubled exemptions and a tax is payable, the gift is kept out of the higher "brackets" of the tax scale.

For example, suppose a man puts $200,000 into a trust for benefit of his son. If he were taxed for the whole gift, his tax would be $30,600. But by splitting the gift so that he reports $100,000 and his wife does the same, the aggregate tax is only $17,190.

THE RULES FOR SPLITTING GIFTS

DATE OF GIFT IS WHAT COUNTS: A husband and wife can't split a gift unless they were married to each other at the time the gift was made. If they got married in June, for instance, they can't split gifts made earlier in the year. If they are divorced during the year or one of them dies, they can't split any gifts made afterward.

REMARRIAGE: Anyone who remarries during a certain year can't under any circumstances split a gift made earlier in that year.

YOU MUST SPLIT ALL OR NONE: If a husband and wife decide they want to split a certain gift, they must likewise split all other gifts they made that year while married to each other.

YOU HAVE A NEW CHOICE EACH YEAR: A husband and wife who decide to split their gifts in 1954 can report their gifts separately in 1955. Whatever they do in one year doesn't bind them in following years.

Both must consent: Gifts can't be split unless the husband and wife agree on the question.

Consents must be shown on returns: The husband and wife don't have to come to a decision about splitting their gifts until they file gift tax returns after the year has ended. The returns have spaces for consenting to have gifts split. If only one of the spouses needs to file a return, both must consent on the one return that is filed. If each files a return (the usual situation), each can consent on his own return or the consent of both can be shown on one of the returns. However, the Treasury asks that, if possible, both consents be given on both returns.

The general rule is that, to be effective, the consents must be signified on or before April 15 following the year in which the gifts were made (March 15, if gifts were made before 1955). There's an exception to the rule where no returns are filed before the fifteenth.

If you change your mind: If returns filed before April 15 do not show a consent, the husband and wife can file amended returns up to the fifteenth and consent on them to have their gifts split. If returns filed before April 15 do show consents, either the husband or wife can withdraw his or her consent up to the fifteenth.

Tax can be collected from either: Where a husband and wife have consented to have their gifts split, the government can collect that year's tax from either one of them.

LOOKING A LONG WAY AHEAD TO SAVE TAXES

When a husband and wife split their gifts, they often save thousands of dollars of gift tax. What if one of them dies before it's time to file gift tax returns for a certain year? Can his or her executor make a valid consent to have the gifts split?

So far as the Federal tax authorities are concerned, he can. The gift tax law specifically provides for the situation.

But the executor may find that, without permission in the will, he isn't justified in giving his consent. Under State law, perhaps, the estate can't become liable for the tax on the surviving spouse's gifts. The chance to save tax, therefore, might be lost.

The next time you are talking to your lawyer about your will, ask him if anything should be said in the will on this point.

(Give some thought to income taxes too. For the final year, will your executor be in a position to file a joint Federal income tax return with your wife or husband? The income tax law says he can; but is that enough?)

EXAMPLE: *A man and his wife elect to split their gifts for 1955. Several years later, after they have separated, the government finds that the husband made gifts in 1955 that were not reported. Additional tax is due.* The government can collect all of this additional tax, with penalties and interest, from the wife.

NONRESIDENT ALIENS CAN'T SPLIT GIFTS: Suppose either the husband or the wife is a nonresident of the United States and an alien. The couple can't split the gifts.

12

How to Figure Your Tax

> ▶ *Finding your net gifts. The gift tax rates. If no gift tax returns have ever been filed— what to do.*

Let's say you make some gifts in 1955 and want to find out how much tax you owe on account of them.

First, make a list of the gifts. For each gift, show the market value of the property at the date of the gift.

Second, group the gifts according to the donees and show a total for each donee.

For instance, if your original list is:

To wife	$1,000
" son	5,000
" wife	9,000
" son	35,000
Total	$50,000

change it to this:

To wife	$10,000
" son	40,000
Total	$50,000

Third, if you are married and if you and your spouse are going to split the gifts to others, reduce the total by half the value of the gifts to others.

EXAMPLE: Total gifts $50,000
         Less half the value of gifts to son   20,000
         Balance $30,000

But then you must treat as *your* gifts half the value of any gifts your wife or husband made to others. Let's assume she or he gave $10,000 to a daughter, so you add $5,000.

EXAMPLE: Balance of gifts $30,000
         Plus half the value of gifts made
           by spouse to daughter   5,000
         Balance $35,000

Fourth, reduce the balance by the annual exclusions. The rule is that the first $3,000 of gifts to any person in any year is exempt (except that there is no exemption if the gift is of a future interest).

EXAMPLE: Balance of gifts $35,000
         Less $3,000 exclusions for gifts to
           wife, son, and daughter   9,000
         Balance $26,000

Fifth, reduce the balance by your deductions. There are three possible deductions:
   (1) the charitable deduction (for gifts to charities, etc.),
   (2) the marital deduction (for half the value of gifts to wife or husband),
   (3) the $30,000 lifetime exemption (if it hasn't all been used in earlier years).
In our example, there are no gifts to charities, so there's no charitable deduction. Assume that all the lifetime exemption has been used in earlier years, so there's no deduction on that account. That leaves only the marital deduction, which would be $5,000.

EXAMPLE: Balance of gifts $26,000
    Less marital deduction (half of
     the $10,000 gifts to wife)   5,000
      Taxable gifts for 1955 $21,000

Sixth, add to your taxable gifts for 1955 the total taxable gifts for all previous years, back to June 6, 1932. Let's assume these earlier taxable gifts are $34,000.

EXAMPLE: Taxable gifts for 1955 $21,000
    Taxable gifts for earlier years   34,000
     Taxable gifts for all years $55,000

Explanation—Sixth Step: Here is how you can find the amount of taxable gifts for earlier years:

Get out a copy of the latest gift tax return you have filed. If that return was for 1943 or any later year, the figure for "Total net gifts" or "Total taxable gifts," on the face of the return, is what you want now. It is a cumulative figure. If your returns have been properly prepared, it takes into account all necessary adjustments.

If the latest gift tax return was for 1942 or before, you probably will have to make an adjustment to the "Total net gifts" figure. The adjustment is to allow for any excess lifetime exemption you may have taken on your old returns.

By "excess" lifetime exemption we mean the excess over $30,000. The lifetime exemption is now $30,000. Before 1943 it was higher ($40,000 from 1936 to 1942, inclusive, and $50,000 from 1932 to 1935). If you made gifts before 1943 you may have claimed more than $30,000 of exemption, and in that case you must now "give back" to the government the excess. You do this by increasing the total net gifts for earlier years.

Giving back some of the exemption in this way does not increase the amount of gifts taxed in the current year. It sometimes has the effect, however, of boosting the current-year gifts into a higher tax bracket.

Seventh, figure the tax, from the table below, on:

Your taxable gifts for all years $

and

Your taxable gifts for years before 1955 $

Subtracting the tax on the before-1955 gifts from the tax on all gifts, you get:

Your tax for 1955, the current year $

The Rates

(1) TAXABLE GIFTS	(2) TAX ON AMOUNT IN COLUMN (1)	(3) RATE OF TAX ON NEXT BRACKET (PER CENT)
$ —	$ —	$2\frac{1}{4}$
5,000	$112\frac{1}{2}$	$5\frac{1}{4}$
10,000	375	$8\frac{1}{4}$
20,000	1,200	$10\frac{1}{2}$
30,000	2,250	$13\frac{1}{2}$
40,000	3,600	$16\frac{1}{2}$
50,000	5,250	$18\frac{3}{4}$
60,000	7,125	21
100,000	15,525	$22\frac{1}{2}$
250,000	49,275	24
500,000	109,275	$26\frac{1}{4}$
750,000	174,900	$27\frac{3}{4}$

(1) TAXABLE GIFTS	(2) TAX ON AMOUNT IN COLUMN (1)	(3) RATE OF TAX ON NEXT BRACKET (PER CENT)
1,000,000	244,275	29¼
1,250,000	317,400	31½
1,500,000	396,150	33¾
2,000,000	564,900	36¾
2,500,000	748,650	39¾
3,000,000	947,400	42
3,500,000	1,157,400	44¼
4,000,000	1,378,650	47¼
5,000,000	1,851,150	50¼
6,000,000	2,353,650	52½
7,000,000	2,878,650	54¾
8,000,000	3,426,150	57
10,000,000	4,566,150	57¾

EXAMPLE:

Tax on $55,000 (taxable gifts for all years) $6,187.50
Tax on $34,000 (taxable gifts for earlier years)   2,790.00
Tax on $21,000 (taxable gifts for current year) $3,397.50

WHY THE TAX IS FIGURED IN THIS ROUNDABOUT WAY

Would it not be much simpler if the taxpaper could just match his current year's gifts directly against a table of rates? It would. But in that case, of course, each year's gifts would be taxed at the lowest rates of the scale. Under the present gift tax scheme, each year's gifts are piled on top of earlier gifts. As the years go by the taxpayer finds that the tax on his gifts becomes increasingly burdensome.

WHAT DOES A MAN DO IF HE HAS NEVER FILED A GIFT TAX RETURN?

"My situation is different," a taxpayer may say to himself. "I've never filed any gift tax returns at all. But I think now that I should have, considering that for the past ten or fifteen years I've been putting a lot of property in joint names of myself and my wife. How can I make a rough estimate of what I owe?"

A taxpayer in this situation has a great deal of company. There's nothing like the gift tax for getting a person delinquent in his tax liabilities. It's a tax that is easily overlooked.

The best advice to such a taxpayer is that he ask his attorney or accountant to compute the tax he owes. It is quite an arithmetic problem, if the gifts go back many years.

But if a taxpayer wants to try to figure it out himself, he will find a section later in this book that may help. It is "How to Figure Gift Tax for Past Years," page 278.

It has all the old rates and exemptions, back to the start of the present gift tax system in 1932.

In this respect the gift tax is like the estate tax. The gift tax is a graduated tax on gifts during life, just as the estate tax is a graduated tax on gifts at death. Historically, the gift tax is a supplement to the estate tax; it was meant to plug the estate tax loophole that existed in the opportunity to give one's property away during life. So, in order to relate the gift tax rates to the estate tax rates in some logical fashion, the gift tax was planned as a "once-in-a-lifetime" tax, though returns must be filed and some of the tax paid as the gifts are made.

Part Four

WHAT YOU CAN DO ABOUT IT...STANDARD METHODS OF SAVING TAX

13

Avoid a "Second" Tax on Your Property

▶ *How your plans will affect the taxes payable in other estates: Outright bequests under your will. Leaving property in trust under a will. Control of trust by the beneficiary. Trust need not be inflexible. Life insurance. Jointly held property.*

Part Two of this book shows how you can make an estimate of what the Federal estate tax will be on your estate.

There are a number of things you may be able to do to reduce that tax.

Perhaps, if you are married, you can change your will and get a bigger "marital deduction." You may find it practical to give some of your property to your family while you are living, so that your estate at death will be smaller. Or you can leave some of your property for charities, etc., and be rewarded by a smaller estate tax.

Those steps and a number of other ways to reduce the tax in your estate are taken up in the following chapters.

This chapter doesn't deal with the tax on your estate. Instead, it shows how you can prevent a tax on your property when the persons to whom you leave it die.

It shows how you can eliminate a "second" or a "third" tax on your property. The "first" tax—the tax on your estate—will come in for attention later.

If that seems to be "putting the cart before the horse," remember this: *the steps you take to save tax in your own estate are likely to affect the amount of taxes in your beneficiaries' estates.*

If you don't know just how the taxes in your beneficiaries' estates are affected by your plans, you are operating in the dark.

It would be poor economy for you to do something that would cut the tax in your estate by $10,000 if, as a result, you lost the chance to save $20,000 tax in your wife's or husband's estate.

There are a number of ways you might lose that chance. It all depends on how you distribute your property.

So let's take a look on the other side of the fence and see where you're going to land. *Then* come back and consider the ways and means of clearing the hurdle—the tax on your own estate.

OUTRIGHT BEQUESTS UNDER YOUR WILL

Hesitate before leaving a large amount of money or property outright to someone who has no special skill in financial matters. You may be taking the risk that the fund will soon be lost or squandered.

If it isn't lost or squandered, your beneficiary may pass it on at his death to someone you would never choose as a beneficiary.

These are powerful arguments against outright bequests in a will. However, they are hardly within the scope of taxes. The tax disadvantage connected with outright bequests is this:

If you leave property outright to someone, it usually will be taxed as a part of his estate when he dies, if he still has it then.

This is generally so, though the property has already been taxed at your death. The only exception is where the beneficiary survives you by less than ten years; and even then the exception does not apply to all the property inherited from a spouse who dies in 1948 or later.

THREE TAXES TAKE $70,000 OF $200,000 ESTATE

What is the Federal estate tax on a $200,000 estate? The rate tables say it is $31,500. But see what happens when that $200,000 estate passes—by outright bequests—through the hands of several owners:

The First Tax: Mr. A dies at an advanced age leaving his $200,000 estate outright to his son. Tax	$31,500
The Second Tax: The son dies more than ten years later, leaving what's left of the money ($168,500) to *his* son. Tax	$22,500
The Third Tax: If the grandson should die after another ten years, leaving the dwindling fund to his brothers and sisters, the tax would be	$16,400
Total Federal estate tax	$70,400

Less than $130,000 would be left of the original $200,000. State inheritance taxes, if taken into account, would make the picture all the darker. And so would executors' commissions and other estate costs.

Considering taxes, outright gifts under your will can be a decidedly expensive means of transmitting property to your heirs.

LEAVING PROPERTY IN TRUST UNDER A WILL

Now suppose the man in the example above, instead of leaving his $200,000 estate outright to his son, had provided in his will as follows:

My estate, after payment of debts, taxes, and expenses, is to be held in trust for my son John, with income payable to him while he lives. After his death the trust is to continue for his son George. And at George's death the trust is to end and the property paid to [certain named persons].

In that case there would be only one tax—the $31,500 payable at Mr. A's death. The second and third taxes, at the son's and the grandson's deaths, would be eliminated.

The trust could save nearly $40,000 of Federal tax.

There would also be a probable saving of State inheritance taxes. There might be still another saving from the avoidance of executors' commissions and estate costs in the second and third estates, although this particular saving would be offset somewhat by the trustee's commissions.

Leaving property *in trust* under your will is a perfectly legitimate way to eliminate taxes at the death of your beneficiary. Compared to leaving property outright, a trust arrangement usually is economical. Less money goes to the tax collector, more to your ultimate heirs.

THE BENEFICIARY MUST NOT CONTROL THE TRUST

When you are thinking of leaving property in trust under your will, you may say to yourself: "I can't see into the future. My beneficiary may run into an emergency of some kind and need the principal. Can I give her the right to withdraw the principal?"

Perhaps you can. But if you do—if you give the beneficiary the right to take all the principal at any time—then the trust saves no taxes at the beneficiary's death. The property in the trust will be taxed as a part of her estate, just as though she owned it outright.

The same would be true if you should provide that the

beneficiary should have the right to name the persons to receive the principal at her death. This is called a power of appointment. If the power is unrestricted—if the beneficiary can make a will, for instance, and give the trust property to anyone she chooses—then the property in the trust will be considered, for Federal estate tax purposes, as a part of her estate.

YET THE TRUST NEED NOT BE INFLEXIBLE

"How far can I go, if I want the trust to save taxes?" the person having his will drawn says. "I don't want to tie up the property too hard and fast."

You can give *the trustee* authority to pay some of the principal to the beneficiary. This is a very common provision in wills. Inasmuch as it is not the beneficiary who has the right, the trust can be of the tax-saving type. In other words, the trustee's discretionary power to pay out principal does not make the trust taxable at the beneficiary's death.

Or, you might consider giving the beneficiary a "limited power of appointment." For instance, you could provide that the beneficiary, by her will, shall have the right to allot the principal in any way she may choose among your children and grandchildren.* Such a right on her part—even though she makes use of it and names certain of the children or grandchildren to receive the principal—does not cause the property in the trust to be taxed as a part of her estate.

---

* The important point is that the beneficiary must not have the right to appoint the property to herself, her estate, or the creditors of herself or her estate. If she cannot so appoint the property, it does not matter how large a group of persons she *can* appoint to; the power is "limited."

LIFE INSURANCE TOO CAN ESCAPE A SECOND TAX

Insurance that is payable to your estate—to your executor, that is—becomes merged with your other property. Under your will it passes to your legatees either outright or in trust. If it goes outright, it becomes the property of your legatee and will be taxed as a part of his or her estate. But if you leave it in trust, you can avoid a second tax on it, as in the case of other property passing under your will.

What about life insurance that is payable direct to your beneficiary? Is there anything you can do to avoid a Federal tax on this when your beneficiary dies?

There are two possibilities. *First,* you can have the insurance paid under one of the optional methods of settlement that are available under the policies. *Second,* you can have the insurance paid to an insurance trust.

THE OPTIONAL METHODS OF SETTLEMENT: Almost every life insurance policy gives the policyholder a choice among several methods of having the proceeds paid to, or held for, the beneficiary. If you will read your policies, you will probably find that you can have the proceeds:

(a) paid to the beneficiary in one lump sum; or
(b) kept on deposit with the insurance company, with interest payable to your beneficiary; or
(c) paid as a "life income" to the beneficiary, the payments to continue at least for ten, fifteen, or twenty years after your death; or
(d) paid in monthly installments during a certain fixed period after your death.

The first method, a, needs little comment. The money immediately becomes the beneficiary's and it ordinarily will be taxed as a part of her estate, if she still has it when she dies. It is no more likely to escape a "second" tax than is money you leave outright under your will.

Under method b the insurance proceeds will be taxed as a part of the beneficiary's estate if she has the right to withdraw the sum on deposit, or if it will be payable to her estate, or if she has the right to name the persons to receive it at her death. Otherwise—where you have given the beneficiary no rights except the right to receive the interest—there is no tax at the beneficiary's death.

Under methods c and d the insurance proceeds are set up in a decreasing fund. The longer the beneficiary lives, the less there will be payable by the insurance company after her death. If the beneficiary lives long enough, nothing will be payable.

> If the beneficiary spends the payments she receives during her lifetime, it is only the payments, if any, made by the insurance company after her death that could be penalized by a second tax.

As to those payments, if there are any, here is the rule: Their discounted value as of the time the beneficiary dies will be taxed as a part of the beneficiary's estate if:

(1) the beneficiary had the right while living to "commute" the payments—that is, to obtain their cash value from the insurance company, or

(2) the payments are made to the beneficiary's estate, or

(3) the beneficiary had the right to name the persons to receive them.

INSURANCE TRUSTS: Many policyholders make their insurance payable to insurance trusts they have established. For example, a policyholder enters into an "insurance trust agreement" with a trustee—usually a bank or trust company—and gives instructions like this:

> You are to receive the proceeds of my insurance policies when I die. Invest this money and pay the income to my wife while she lives. Pay her some of the principal too if, in your opinion, she needs it in case of illness or some other emergency. At her death, distribute the principal among my children who are then living . . . [etc.]

When the wife dies, will there be a second tax? In other words, will the property in the insurance trust be treated as a part of her estate in figuring her Federal estate tax?

It all depends on the rights and powers the policyholder gives the beneficiary. It's exactly like a trust made by will.

If the beneficiary can withdraw the principal or can name the persons to receive the principal at her death, then the trust property *will* be included in her estate. There will be a second tax.

If the beneficiary has no such rights, the trust property will not be taxed in her estate. (The *trustee's* power to pay out principal to the beneficiary in emergencies would not cause a tax.)

An insurance trust, therefore, is a practical way to eliminate a second tax on insurance proceeds. A third tax could be saved too. For instance, the policyholder might have the income of a trust paid to his wife while she lives, then to his daughter while she lives; and with principal eventually payable to his grandchildren. Under these circumstances the property in the trust would escape tax at the daughter's death as well as at the wife's. The trust would by-pass two estates.

JOINTLY HELD PROPERTY

Suppose you and somebody else own property as "joint

tenants with right of survivorship" or as "tenants by the entirety." The entire property passes to the other person if you die before he does.

The same thing happens in the case of joint bank accounts and U. S. Savings Bonds registered in names of co-owners.

In these cases the full value of the property might be taxed in your estate. (It would unless your executor could prove certain facts regarding who paid for the property or deposited the money. See Chapter 2.)

Would it be taxed again when the survivor dies?

Yes, probably. It's like an outright bequest in your will. The only circumstances under which it might not be taxed would be where your co-owner survives you by less than ten years (and even this exception doesn't always apply if the co-owner is your wife or husband).

Therefore, if you want to keep property in joint names, there's nothing you can do to eliminate the second tax.

SUMMARY

Let's see if there is a general rule that's good for all kinds of property and for all kinds of situations.

You can generally eliminate a second tax on property you leave to a beneficiary by tying up the property, so that your beneficiary can't freely spend the principal while living or give the principal to anyone he wishes at his death.

You can let the beneficiary have the income. And you can authorize a trustee to pay him some of the principal. You can even give the beneficiary *some* control over who gets the principal at his death.

But don't let the beneficiary do as he pleases with the property.

If you do, there will be a second tax.

14

Split Your Estate with Your Wife or Husband

> ▶ *Tax saved in your estate by marital deduction.
> But marital deduction may not always be advis-
> able. How to split estate to best advantage;
> cases: Husband owns everything. Husband owns
> everything and wants to tie up everything in
> trust. Husband owns everything and carries life
> insurance. Husband owns everything, carries
> life insurance, and owns joint property with
> wife. Husband has $200,000, wife has $100,000.
> Husband has $200,000, wife has $200,000.
> Husband has $100,000, wife has $200,000.*

At the start of the preceding chapter we said you might be able to reduce the Federal estate tax on your estate by arranging to get the largest possible marital deduction.

A marital deduction, you will recall (see Chapter 4), is allowed for the value of property left to a surviving wife or husband. It can't be more than half the adjusted gross estate (the gross estate less debts and expenses, usually); and the property must be left to the surviving wife or husband outright or in one of several other specified ways.

The marital deduction makes a tremendous difference in the tax. Look at the following table:

(1)	(2)	(3)
IF YOUR ESTATE, LESS DEBTS AND EXPENSES, IS	WITH *No* MARITAL DEDUCTION, THE FEDERAL TAX ON YOUR ESTATE WILL BE	WITH THE *Largest Possible* MARITAL DEDUCTION, THE TAX WILL BE
$ 80,000	$ 1,600	$ 0
100,000	4,800	0
125,000	10,700	75
150,000	17,500	1,050
175,000	24,400	2,650
200,000	31,500	4,800
250,000	45,300	10,700
300,000	59,100	17,500
400,000	87,700	31,500
500,000	116,500	45,300
750,000	191,800	80,500
1,000,000	270,300	116,500
2,000,000	626,600	270,300
4,000,000	1,522,400	626,600

(The estate, in column 1, has not been reduced by the $60,000 exemption. In columns 2 and 3 the Federal tax is the net amount payable, after taking off the credit for State taxes.)

All you have to do to get the largest possible marital deduction for your estate is to leave at least half of all your property to your wife or husband in a certain way—by an outright bequest under your will, for instance.

WATCH OUT FOR THE SECOND TAX

But now we are going to confuse you by saying that it isn't

always best for your estate to get the full marital deduction. It may be advisable for your estate to get no marital deduction at all.

Why is that so? Because, if you leave property to your spouse in such a way that your estate gets a marital deduction for it, *that property is likely to be taxed in your spouse's estate.*

In other words, the second tax looms ahead. This second tax may be more than the tax you save in your estate by using the marital deduction.

"SPLIT INCOMES"

This problem of when the marital deduction should be used and when it shouldn't, can be clarified by a comparison with income taxes.

The Revenue Act of 1948 brought the "split-income" principle into the Federal tax system. Under this principle, if a husband has a large income and his wife has no income at all, they can, by filing a joint return, have the husband's income taxed as though each earned half.

That saves tax, of course, because it keeps the income out of the high brackets of the tax scale.

It will readily be seen that this split-income principle is a big help where one spouse's income is much larger than the other's.

But it is no help at all if their incomes are already equal. They could do just about as well by filing separate returns, which they have always been permitted to do.

"SPLIT ESTATES"

The Revenue Act of 1948 added the same kind of a splitting principle to *estate taxes.*

Under this principle, if a husband has a large amount of property and his wife has little or no property of her own, he can have his property taxed much as though he owned half and she owned half. In effect, he can split his property —or, at least, the taxation of his property—between two estates. In doing so, of course, he saves estate tax.

▶ Because of the $60,000 exemption that each estate is entitled to and the rising scale of rates, it is always cheaper to have a certain sum divided between two estates than to have it all taxed in one.

This new split-estates principle is vitally important where one spouse owns much more property than does the other. It can save them thousands of dollars of tax.

But it offers less advantage—perhaps none at all—if the husband's and wife's estates are already equal. Under those circumstances they have always been able—by means of trusts under their wills—to have each estate taxed for half the total property and no more.

HOW TO SPLIT YOUR ESTATE

The device by which a married person can split his *income*, for tax purposes, is the joint return.

The device by which a married person can split his *estate*, for tax purposes, is the marital deduction.

Looked at in this way, the marital deduction is not merely a means of saving tax in your estate. It is a means of equalizing your and your spouse's taxable estates.

If you can do that—if you can arrange matters so that the amount actually taxed in your estate will be approximately equal to the amount taxed in your spouse's—then you will come close to achieving the most economical way of passing your property on to your family.

Here are illustrations of how it can be done:

HUSBAND OWNS EVERYTHING

Mr. A owns property valued at $200,000. Mrs. A has little or no property of her own.

He knows that if the whole $200,000 should be taxed in either estate, there would be a large Federal tax. (It would be $31,500.)

What he wants is to have $100,000 taxed when he dies and $100,000 taxed when Mrs. A dies later. (In that case the total Federal tax in the two estates would be less than $10,000.)

So in his will he provides that HALF of his estate, after debts and expenses are paid, shall be given to Mrs. A outright.

That entitles his estate to a marital deduction of about $100,000, leaving only $100,000 to be taxed.

He provides that the other half of his estate, less taxes, shall be tied up in a trust for Mrs. A. She is to receive the income for life; and the trustee can pay her some of the principal if, in the trustee's opinion, she needs it in an emergency. But she will not have the right to withdraw principal whenever she wishes. Neither can she name the persons to receive the principal at her death.

The property in this trust will not be taxed as a part of Mrs. A's estate when she dies. The only property that will be taxed at her death will be the $100,000 she receives outright (if she hasn't spent it meanwhile).

RESULT: Mr. A splits the taxation of his $200,000 between his and his wife's estates. In doing so, he can expect to save about $20,000 in Federal tax.

HUSBAND OWNS EVERYTHING AND WANTS TO TIE UP EVERYTHING IN TRUST

Mr. B's situation is exactly like Mr. A's except that he (Mr. B) objects to giving his wife $100,000 outright. He wants his whole $200,000 estate to be held in trust.

So in his will he establishes TWO trusts.

Trust No. 1 is for half his estate, after debts and expenses are paid. Mrs. B is to receive the trust income for life, and she also is to have the unrestricted right to name the persons to receive the principal at her death.

That entitles Mr. B's estate to a marital deduction of about $100,000, leaving only $100,000 to be taxed.

Trust No. 2 is for the other half of his estate, less taxes. It is like Trust No. 1, except that Mrs. B does not have the right to name the persons to receive the principal.

The property in this trust will not be taxed as a part of Mrs. B's estate. Only Trust No. 1 will be taxed at her death.

RESULT: Like Mr. A, Mr. B splits his estate and can expect to save about $20,000 in Federal tax.

If Mr. B wants to authorize the trustee to pay some of the principal to Mrs. B in emergencies, he should give that authorization with respect to Trust No. 1. If Mrs. B receives and spends some of the principal from that trust, less will remain to be taxed at her death.

HUSBAND OWNS EVERYTHING AND CARRIES LIFE INSURANCE

Mr. C owns property valued at $150,000; and he also carries $50,000 insurance on his life. Mrs. C has little or no property of her own.

Mr. C's problem is to leave $100,000 to his wife in such a way as to entitle his estate to a marital deduction; and to leave about as much to her, or for her benefit, in such a way that it will not be included in her taxable estate.

One Method: In his will he could provide that $100,000 should be given Mrs. C outright (or held in trust for her, with the unrestricted right on her part to name the persons to receive the principal at her death). This would entitle his estate to a $100,000 marital deduction.

He could tie up the rest of his estate and all of the insurance so that they would not be taxed at her death. The estate funds could be held in trust. The insurance proceeds could be put under one of the "options" or made payable to an insurance trust.

Another Method: Perhaps a better way would be for Mr. C to provide in his will that $100,000, less all taxes on his estate, should be held in trust for Mrs. C with no right on her part to name the persons to receive the principal at her death.

Then the rest of his estate and all of the insurance proceeds could be given to Mrs. C outright (or in any other way that would entitle Mr. C's estate to a marital deduction).

RESULT OF EITHER METHOD: Mr. C would split the taxation of his $200,000 between his and Mrs. C's estates. He could expect to save about $20,000 in Federal tax.

HUSBAND OWNS EVERYTHING, CARRIES LIFE INSURANCE, AND OWNS PROPERTY JOINTLY WITH WIFE

Mr. D owns $50,000 of property in his own name, and he carries $50,000 of insurance.

In addition, he and his wife hold $100,000 worth of securities and real estate in their joint names with right of survivorship. Mr. D paid for this property, so it will all be included in his estate for Federal tax purposes.

GETTING THE MARITAL DEDUCTION CHEAPLY

If you want your life insurance paid to your wife or husband as a life income under one of the "options" set forth in the policies,

> you can get a marital deduction for the full amounts of the policies (if you give your spouse enough control over the payments),

> and yet only a small part of those amounts, or perhaps none at all, may ever be taxed in your spouse's estate.

This is because, under these options, the insurance proceeds are set up in a decreasing fund. The longer the beneficiary lives, the less there will be payable after her death. If the beneficiary lives long enough, nothing will be payable.

It is only this decreasing amount that would be taxed in the beneficiary's estate (assuming she spends her installments as she receives them). Very often there will be nothing whatever to be taxed.

This isn't exactly a case of "eating your cake and having it too." The real reason for the small tax, or the absence of tax, when the surviving spouse dies is that she has used up some of her capital.

But it shows that you should look to your insurance as one of the best sources of a marital deduction for your estate.

Mrs. D owns no property in her own name.

If Mr. D wants to split his estate so that $100,000 will be taxed when he dies and $100,000 when Mrs. D dies, there is only one thing he can do:

He must tie up both the property passing under his will

and the insurance in such a way that neither will be taxed as a part of Mrs. D's estate.

He must do that because the $100,000 of jointly owned property *will* be taxed in Mrs. D's estate. It passes to her automatically when he dies. If he should give her more property, her total estate would be more than $100,000 and the second tax would be needlessly high.

The jointly owned property will entitle Mr. D's estate to the largest possible marital deduction—$100,000. Only $100,-000 will remain to be taxed.

RESULT: Mr. D splits the taxation of the $200,000 and saves about $20,000 in Federal tax.

HUSBAND OWNS $200,000, WIFE OWNS $100,000

Mr. E owns property valued at $200,000. His wife owns property valued at $100,000.

TAX SAVING IN THEORY: The total is $300,000. Mathematically, it might seem, Mr. E should try to have $150,000 taxed when he dies and $150,000 taxed when Mrs. E dies later.

He could accomplish such a result by leaving $50,000 to her outright (or in trust, giving her the income plus the right to name the persons to receive the principal). The rest of his estate he could tie up in trust for Mrs. E so that it would not be taxed in her estate.

Thus, his estate would get a $50,000 marital deduction, reducing it to $150,000. Mrs. E would receive the $50,000 from his estate, and together with the property she already owned it would leave her with an estate of $150,000.

TAX SAVING IN PRACTICE: But notice that Mr. E's estate is not getting the largest possible marital deduction. His estate is $200,000. The government would let him deduct $100,000 if he should leave that much to his wife in the proper way. If he leaves her only $50,000, won't his estate pay a larger tax than it needs to?

"Yes, but by leaving her only $50,000, I'm saving tax in *her* estate," Mr. E says. "I'm equalizing the estates at $150,000."

That is true. But you ought to think twice before you give up the right to the largest possible marital deduction. There's a practical consideration that often upsets the mathematical calculations. It is this:

With the husband's earnings gone, the widow may spend a good deal of her capital.

If Mrs. E should do that, Mr. E wouldn't be "equalizing" the estates by leaving her only $50,000.

EXAMPLE:

His estate	$200,000	Her estate	$100,000
Less marital deduction	50,000	Plus amount received from his estate	50,000
Taxed at his death	$150,000		$150,000
		Less $50,000 of capital spent during widowhood	50,000
		Taxed at her death	$100,000

ARGUMENTS FOR THE FULL DEDUCTION: Obviously Mr. E can't know how much capital Mrs. E will spend. She may survive him many years or, on the other hand, only a few months. She may or may not be able to get along on her income alone.

Mr. E can, however, figure how much Federal tax would be saved in his estate by an extra $50,000 deduction. It is

GETTING EXACTLY THE RIGHT AMOUNT OF
MARITAL DEDUCTION FOR YOUR ESTATE

If the wife has no property of her own, it usually is best for
the husband to leave her exactly half his adjusted gross
estate in a way that entitles his estate to the marital deduction.

*If she receives less, the husband's estate sacrifices some of
the marital deduction. If she receives more, her estate is
likely to be needlessly taxed.*

Sometimes it is difficult to phrase the husband's will so
that the wife gets exactly half the adjusted gross estate.
There may be life insurance and jointly owned property
to be taken into consideration; and the value of the various
assets of his estate at death certainly can't be known at
the time the will is drawn.

This is a problem for the lawyer who draws the husband's will. Perhaps he will use the words of the Federal
tax law, "adjusted gross estate," in describing the bequest
to the wife. Or he may avoid that term and fix the amount
of the bequest by some other means.

When the Wife Has Property Too: Fortunately, if the
wife has a considerable amount of property of her own, the
precise amount of her bequest isn't so important from a tax
viewpoint.

$12,700. If this much less tax were paid by his estate, the
amount left for the widow would be just that much more.
Interest or other income would be earned on the extra money
so long as the widow lived.

Considering these facts, along with the possibility that
Mrs. E will consume some of her capital, Mr. E might wisely

For example, a man is worth $300,000, his wife $100,000. The total is $400,000, so it might seem best if $200,000 could be taxed when he dies and $200,000 when she dies. That means that he should leave her $100,000 in a way that qualifies for the marital deduction.

Now what if the bequest turns out to be $110,000, or $125,000, or even $150,000? Her taxable estate would be pushed over $200,000, while somewhat less than $200,000 would be taxed in his estate. The estates wouldn't be equal.

But it happens that the top rate of Federal tax on estates between $200,000 and $300,000 isn't any higher than on estates between $160,000 and $200,000.

In fact, after you take off the credit for State tax, the top rate is a little lower on the over-$200,000 estates.

So in this particular situation—and in many others where the wife owns property—the amounts taxed in the two estates don't need to be exactly equal. The husband should not leave *more* than half his adjusted gross estate to her in a way that qualifies for the marital deduction. But up to that maximum figure there usually is some leeway, and there may be no harm in stating the bequest to his wife simply as a certain fraction of the residue of his estate.

decide to leave as much as $100,000 outright to Mrs. E, thus obtaining the largest possible marital deduction for his estate.

RESULT: Mr. E, by means of the full marital deduction, reduces the Federal tax on his $200,000 estate by $26,700 (from $31,500 to $4,800). In doing so, he adds to the amount of property that will be taxed in his wife's estate later on. But his widow will have the use of the $26,700 while she lives; and, besides, she may spend a good deal of her money and not have such a large estate to be taxed after all.

Under the circumstances Mr. E's plans are sound.

THE WIFE'S PLANS: If Mrs. E should die first, the Federal tax on her $100,000 estate would be only $4,800. It would be poor economy for her to reduce that tax by means of the marital deduction; she would almost surely increase the tax in her husband's estate by more than she would save. Therefore, she should leave all her estate in trust for her husband in such a way that it will not be taxed as a part of his estate.

HUSBAND HAS $200,000, WIFE HAS $200,000

Mr. F owns property valued at $200,000. Mrs. F owns an equal amount of property.

They see the wisdom of leaving their property in trust under their wills. For example, Mrs. F's will leaves everything in trust for Mr. F. He is to receive the income while he lives, and after his death the principal is to be distributed among their children. Under this trust Mr. F does *not* have the right to change the disposition of the principal.

Thus, Mrs. F's $200,000 will be fully taxed at her death; but none of it will be taxed as a part of her husband's estate should he survive her.

Mr. F's will, however, is a little different. It leaves $50,000 to Mrs. F outright, with only the remaining $150,000, less taxes, held in trust for Mrs. F. Under this trust Mrs. F will *not* have the right to name the persons to receive the principal.

Why does Mr. F leave $50,000 to his wife outright? In doing so, of course, he reduces the amount taxed in his estate to $150,000 and raises the amount taxed in his wife's estate to $250,000. He makes the two estates decidedly unequal.

Unlike Mr. E in the preceding example, Mr. F does not expect his widow to spend any of her capital. But he does think it likely that she will survive him ten, fifteen, or twenty years, inasmuch as she is considerably younger than he is. He knows that whatever amount of tax he can save in his estate by means of the marital deduction will be just that much more capital available to his widow for the rest of her life.

A $50,000 marital deduction will reduce the Federal tax on his estate by $14,000. At 4 per cent the tax saved will yield the widow more than $500 income per year. Mr. F believes that it's better to reduce his tax and give her this added income, even though in doing so he might increase the tax on his widow's estate by somewhat more than the $14,000 he saves in his own.

In this particular case the *Federal* tax on the widow's estate would not be raised by as much as $14,000. But Mr. F takes the inheritance tax of his State into consideration too. He finds that, considering both State and Federal taxes, he's increasing his widow's tax by a little more than he saves in his own estate.

RESULT: Mr. F deliberately uses the marital deduction to make the amounts taxed in his and his wife's estates unequal. Even so, he does not appreciably increase the total tax payable by the two estates; *and he adds $500 per year to his widow's income.*

HUSBAND HAS $100,000, WIFE HAS $200,000

Mr. G is worth $100,000, his wife $200,000.

The Federal tax on his $100,000 estate will be only $4,800. If he should reduce that tax by leaving property to his wife so as to qualify for the marital deduction, he would increase the tax in her estate by much more than he would save in his own. So he decides to tie up his entire estate in trust for her, so that the property will not be taxed at her death.

In her will she could leave $50,000 or $100,000 outright to him or for his benefit in a trust that would qualify for the marital deduction. Her remaining property could be tied up for him in trust, so that it would not be taxed in her estate.

However, she decides on a different plan. Her husband has a considerable income from his earnings. If she should die first, he would not need the income from her entire $200,000 estate.

Therefore she leaves only $100,000 for him, with the other $100,000 of her property, less taxes, going direct to the children. The half of her estate left for him can be an outright bequest, or it can be a trust under which he will receive the income for life and will also have the unrestricted right to name the persons to receive the principal at his death.

RESULT: Mr. G does not obtain a marital deduction for his estate.

Mrs. G obtains the largest possible marital deduction for her estate (in the event she dies before he does) and thus may reduce the Federal tax on her estate by $26,700. In doing so, she may increase the tax on his estate by an equal amount. But the reduction would precede the increase, and in the interval $26,700 would yield an income.

YOUR PLANS MAY BE DIFFERENT

In the seven preceding illustrations of how the marital deduction can be used to advantage, little attention has been given to considerations other than taxation.

There are, of course, other important matters to consider in planning your estate. For this reason none of the illustrations should be regarded as a model estate plan.

For instance, if you have $100,000 and your wife has $200,000, as in the case of Mr. and Mrs. G, there may be good and compelling reasons why you should take a course of action quite different from that shown. Perhaps your and your spouse's estates would pay a few thousand dollars more tax than is absolutely necessary. But, compared to the special aims you may wish to achieve in the distribution of your property, the added tax might be of small consequence.

What we are trying to do is merely to "keep you on the right track" so far as taxes are concerned.

TAX SAVINGS—SOMETIMES!

► There is one glaring defect you may have observed in the marital deduction as a means of saving estate taxes: It works to full advantage only if the spouse who has the greater amount of property dies first.

EXAMPLE: *Turn back to the case of Mr. and Mrs. A. He has $200,000 and she has nothing. The marital deduction—by splitting the taxation of the $200,000 between his estate and hers—saves $20,000 in Federal tax, provided he dies before she does.*

If she dies first, there is no marital deduction, no splitting, and no saving. The whole $200,000 will be taxed when Mr. A dies, because (barring a remarriage) there will be no surviving spouse to whom a part of the estate can be left.

This defect may not be quite so serious as it at first appears to be. If the spouse who has the greater amount of property survives, there is no estate tax threat to his own economic security. He will make out. The children or other beneficiaries will bear the burden of a severe tax. But so far as the husband and wife are concerned, the funds upon which they depend for a living are not likely to be seriously depleted by estate tax while either is living.

Nevertheless many persons regard the marital deduction for estate tax as offering only a fifty-fifty chance of splitting an estate for tax purposes.

Is there any other way married couples can split the taxation of their estates—a way that doesn't hinge on which spouse survives?

There is. It is by means of gifts during life. It is discussed in the following chapter.

15

Make Gifts to People Who
Would Eventually Get
Your Property Anyway

> ► *Four reasons why gifts save tax. Husband-to-wife gifts, or vice versa. Gifts by husband or wife to children and grandchildren. Gifts by unmarried persons.*

Ordinarily, if you give some of your property away while you are living, you remove it from your "taxable estate." In other words, there will be no estate tax on it when you die.

There are some important exceptions to this rule. In these exceptional cases the property you have given away is treated —for Federal estate tax purposes—as though it were still yours when you die. That would be so if:

You made a gift in contemplation of death, or
You made gifts by means of a trust and, under the Federal
    tax rules, the gifts "take effect" at or after your death,
You have kept a "string" to the gift in some way.

For an outline of these exceptional situations—situations in which gifts are ineffective in avoiding the estate tax—see Chapter 2.

But let's assume for a moment that you are thinking of making common, ordinary gifts—gifts that will remove the property from your taxable estate.

That means you will have to pay a *gift* tax.

Under these circumstances, can the gifts save tax? Isn't it just a case of avoiding one tax and running into another?

WHY GIFTS SAVE TAX

As a general rule, gifts you make during your lifetime do save tax. There are four reasons for this:

(1) The Federal gift tax rates are lower than the Federal estate tax rates.

(2) By making gifts you divide the taxation of your property between estate tax and gift tax. This is economical, because each tax—the gift tax and estate tax—has its own exemption and its own rising scale of rates. It keeps the property out of the high brackets. This is something like the way income tax can be saved if a certain amount of income is divided between two taxpayers, instead of all being taxed to one of them.

(3) Any gift tax you pay is money that escapes being taxed. Any estate tax that your estate pays is taxed as a part of your estate. Therefore it's better to pay gift tax than estate tax. This may sound like a lot of nonsense, but in it lies an important tax advantage in making lifetime gifts. Suppose a man has $500,000. If he keeps it all till he dies, the whole $500,000 will be taxed—even though an estate tax of well over $100,000 may be paid by his estate. His heirs will get less than $400,000, though $500,000 is taxed. Now if that man had given his heirs $400,000 before he died, there would have been a gift tax on only the $400,000. So even if the gift

tax rates were as high as the estate tax rates, which they aren't, it would be cheaper to pay gift tax.

(4) Sometimes a gift saves income tax. For instance, Mr. A has been helping out his married daughter. Her husband doesn't earn much, and Mr. A feels that she desperately needs the $100 per month that he sends her. That $100 per month, of course, is not an income tax deduction to Mr. A. But he can, in effect, get a deduction for it by giving her stocks and bonds that yield $100 per month. After making the gift his taxable income is $1,200 lower each year, and he might save $500 or $600 a year in income tax, if he has a fairly substantial income. This income tax saving is wholly in addition to the tax saved by paying gift tax instead of estate tax on the property given away.

Saving No. 4, though important, will not be stressed in this chapter. In bringing a third tax—the income tax—into your consideration of gifts, you may lose sight of the very real savings that can be gained in connection with estate and gift taxes. These last two taxes are complicated enough.

GIFTS BY HUSBAND TO WIFE (OR VICE VERSA)

Very well, it may be cheaper—for several reasons—for a man to give his property away while living and pay a gift tax than to keep it and have his estate pay an estate tax.

"But is that true in my case?" a married man asks. "I want my wife to have all my property, or at least the income from it. Wouldn't I save tax if I kept it while living and left it to her by will? That way my estate will get a big marital deduction."

He forgets that there are marital deductions for gift tax (see Chapter 10) as well as for estate tax.

Besides, the estate tax marital deduction isn't sure. Your estate gets it only if you die before your wife does. When you make a gift to your wife while living, on the other hand, you surely will get the marital deduction for gift tax.

So husband-to-wife gifts, or wife-to-husband gifts, generally are advantageous. The gift tax is usually less than the estate tax would be if the property were left by will.

But in all transfers of property between a husband and wife, it's advisable to watch out particularly for a second tax —the tax that may be payable when the survivor of the two dies. A husband and wife plan wisely if they take into consideration their total estate and gift taxes—his plus hers— instead of just the tax that may apply to the property of either.

Considering the total tax bill of the married couple, then, how much of his property should a husband give his wife?

He should give her enough to make her property of equal value to his. If she already has more than he, then she should give something to him.

In other words, they should equalize their estates while living. In Chapter 14 we showed how a married man could save estate tax by making the amount taxable in his estate approximately equal to the amount taxable in his wife's. He can do that by leaving property to his wife so as to qualify for the estate tax marital deduction—provided she survives him. Now here is an improvement on that plan. By equalizing their estates while living—by means of gifts from one to the other—they can save tax no matter which of them survives.

For instance, a man has $200,000 of property, his wife has practically nothing.

He gives her $100,000, paying a gift tax of only $953. (The gift-tax marital deduction helps bring the tax down.)

Then he and she make wills, each leaving his or her estate in trust for the other. These trusts are not the kind that qualify for marital deductions. So when the first one dies, the Federal estate tax on the $100,000 estate will be $4,800.

When the survivor dies, the estate tax in that $100,000 estate likewise will be $4,800.

Altogether, the estate and gift taxes come to only $10,553.

If that man had kept the entire $200,000 while living, the total estate taxes in his and his wife's estates could have been as low as $9,600 if he died first, but no lower than $31,500 if he survived.

By equalizing his and his wife's estates while living, he insured against the much higher tax. The "insurance" cost him only $953 of gift tax.

GIFTS BY HUSBAND OR WIFE TO CHILDREN, GRANDCHILDREN, OR OTHERS

Here we are taking up situations in which a married person makes final, irrevocable gifts to someone other than his spouse.

Gifts like this can be outright or they can be in trust.

Usually these gifts result in a loss of income to the married couple. The husband and wife usually are prepared to get along without the income produced by the securities, the real estate, or whatever property it is that is given away. But that isn't always the case. For instance, a husband puts aside $50,000 in an irrevocable trust, with income going to his wife while she lives. At her death the trust is to end and the principal is to be distributed among their children. In creating this trust, the husband is making gifts to his children (though not of the full $50,000). Gifts like that are among those taken up here.

There is a valuable tax privilege connected with all gifts in this class. As explained in Chapter 11, *they can be split between the husband and wife.*

For example, if a man gives his daughter $10,000, he and his wife can each file a gift tax return reporting a $5,000 gift to the daughter.

This privilege to split the gifts makes for a lower tax in many cases. It does so, generally speaking, wherever one of the spouses—the husband or the wife—owns much more property than does the other. If the two own equal amounts of property, splitting doesn't help much.

Let's see just how much gift tax is saved by splitting in a few typical situations:

GIFT TO ONE CHILD: Mr. Green owns property worth several hundred thousand dollars. Mrs. Green has little or no property of her own.

In 1955 Mr. Green gives his son $100,000 worth of stock in the family business. Mr. Green has not (since June 6, 1932 —the date the present gift tax system started) made any other large gifts, so his $30,000 exemption is intact.

"Then he will pay a gift tax in 1955 on $67,000," you might say offhand. He has the $30,000 lifetime exemption plus a $3,000 annual exclusion. Taking the total $33,000 of exemptions off the $100,000 gift leaves $67,000 to be taxed.

The tax on that $67,000 would be $8,595.

But by splitting the gift, Mr. and Mrs. Green can bring that tax down to $1,905. Here is the arithmetic:

Gift by Mr. Green to son	$100,000
Part considered given by Mr. Green if he and Mrs. Green consent to split the gift	$ 50,000
Less his $30,000 and $3,000 exemptions	33,000
Taxed to Mr. Green	$ 17,000
Mr. Green's tax on the $17,000	$ 952.50
Mrs. Green's tax on $17,000 similarly computed on her gift-tax return	952.50
Total gift tax paid by Mr. and Mrs. Green	$ 1,905.00

Well, wouldn't the results be the same if Mrs. Green had some money of her own? Why did we say the splitting of gifts helps only where the husband and wife have unequal amounts of property?

The point is that, if Mrs. Green owned considerable property, she could have actually made half the gift from her own property. Then—even without this artificial splitting concept that's now in the tax law—her and her husband's tax would have been only $1,905.

Splitting reduces the gift tax of married couples who find it impossible to contribute equally in making gifts.

GIFTS TO TWO OR MORE CHILDREN: Mr. and Mrs. Brown, like the Greens, own their property unequally; Mr. Brown owns practically everything.

They have four children. In 1955 Mr. Brown gives each of them $25,000. Is there any gift tax payable? Not much. Only $540, in fact.

That is because Mr. and Mrs. Brown consent to split each of the $25,000 gifts. To child no. 1, for instance, Mr. Brown is considered to give $12,500, and a $3,000 annual exclusion reduces that to $9,500. Four times $9,500 is $38,000, or $8,000

GIFTS TO CHILDREN BY MEANS OF LIFE INSURANCE—
KEEPING THE GIFT TAX LOW

If you pay a premium on a life insurance or endowment policy that belongs to someone else, you are making a gift to that person. The amount of the gift is the amount of the premium. (See Chapter 8.)

There is no reason why you cannot combine this rule with the splitting principle. For instance, Mr. A, who is married, pays a $6,000 annual premium on an endowment policy owned by his adult son. Mr. and Mrs. A can consent to have the gift treated as though he paid $3,000, she paid $3,000. And if the son is of age, the gifts are wiped out by the annual exclusions.

Suppose the son is under age—a mere child perhaps. There might be some danger here in that the gifts would be considered to be gifts of future interests, as to which no annual $3,000 exclusions are allowed. The question isn't too well settled (although the new provision in the 1954 tax law—see section 2503(c)—may cover the situation in some cases). If you are interested in giving your minor child an endowment policy and paying the premiums on it, talk the matter over with your attorney.

in excess of Mr. Brown's $30,000 lifetime exemption. Mr. Brown's tax on $8,000 is $270.

Mrs. Brown's tax, figured the same way, is $270 also. Altogether they pay $540.

The next year Mr. Brown could give each child an additional $6,000—and neither he nor Mrs. Brown would pay any gift tax. By splitting each $6,000 gift, $3,000 would be considered given by him and $3,000 by her, and those $3,000 gifts would be wiped out by the annual exclusion.

If Mr. Brown wanted to, he could keep on making those annual $6,000 gifts to each child for years—at no cost in gift tax.

GIFTS TO CHILDREN IN TRUST: Parents aren't always willing to let their children have large amounts of property outright. The children may be poor investors or absolutely reckless with money, with the consequent danger that they would spend or lose in short order any large sums given to them.

Or, the children may be mere infants, legally incapable of handling their own funds for years ahead.

For these very good reasons, parents often tie up in trusts any substantial gifts of money or property to their children.

Suppose such a trust is irrevocable. The parent cannot get the money back. There is a gift to the child, children, or other beneficiaries of the trust just as surely as if the money or property had been handed over to those beneficiaries outright (see Chapter 8).

These gifts by means of trusts can be split between the husband and wife, just as can other gifts by the husband or wife.

"But would I save any gift tax by splitting these gifts in trust?" a husband asks. "Aren't there some complications about future interests that prevent the saving?"

There are some complications, all right. But remember this: splitting a gift between husband and wife usually saves tax whether the gift is outright or in trust.

Here is an example of the saving. Don't bother yourself with this example, however, unless you want to understand the mechanics of the tax where gifts in trust are split.

$6,210 Gift Tax Saved by Splitting Gifts in Trust: Take the case

of Mr. Brown, discussed a few paragraphs back. He gave $25,000
—outright—to each of his four children. Let's say now that he
made those gifts *in trust;* that is, he set up a $25,000 irrevocable
trust for each child.

Without splitting the gifts with Mrs. Brown, his gift tax would
have been figured like this:

Deposited in trust for child no. 1	$25,000
Assume the child is thirty-two years old and is entitled to the trust income, as it is collected, during his life. His life estate is considered worth about 70 per cent of the $25,000, or	$17,500
(See table for valuing life estates and remainders, page 270.)	
The rest of the $25,000 is a gift to the person or persons who will receive the principal of the trust when the child dies	$ 7,500
The child's life estate, valued at $17,500, is a present interest, so it can be reduced by a $3,000 annual exclusion	$14,500
The gift of the trust remainder, valued at $7,500, is a future interest, so it cannot be reduced by an annual exclusion	$ 7,500
Mr. Brown's "clear" gifts as to this child's trust	$22,000
His gift as to each of the other three trusts would likewise be $22,000 (assuming the child's life estate in each case is worth at least $3,000)	$66,000
Total "clear" gifts	$88,000
Less lifetime exemption	30,000
Amount taxed	$58,000
Tax	$ 6,750

If Mr. and Mrs. Brown split the gifts, their gift tax is
figured like this:

Mr. Brown's half share of gift of $17,500 life estate to child no. 1	$ 8,750
Less annual exclusion	3,000
	$ 5,750
Mr. Brown's half share of gift of $7,500 trust remainder	3,750
Mr. Brown's "clear" gifts as to this child's trust	$ 9,500
His gift as to each of the other three trusts would likewise be $9,500 (assuming the child's life estate in each case is worth at least $6,000)	$28,500
Mr. Brown's total "clear" gifts	$38,000
Less his lifetime exemption	30,000
Amount taxed to him	$ 8,000
His tax	$ 270
Mrs. Brown's tax, similarly computed	$ 270
Their total tax	$ 540

The Saving:

Tax, gifts not split	$ 6,750
Tax, gifts split	540
SAVED	$ 6,210

THE REAL ADVANTAGE: So far, in discussing gifts by married persons to their children or grandchildren, we have dwelt on the reduction in gift tax that can result from the splitting of gifts between a husband and wife.

But is there any over-all tax economy in making the gifts?

Yes, if the gifts are not in contemplation of death (see Chapter 2). As to parent-to-children gifts, it is usually "cheaper to pay gift tax than estate tax," as is so of gifts generally. A single example will emphasize the advantage.

Mr. Brown, in the example above, gave his children $100,-000 at a cost of only $540 in gift tax.

What if he had kept the $100,000 and left it to his children by his will? What would have been the estate tax on that $100,000?

Well, first of all it depends on the value of his other property. Let's say he had $200,000 of other property, all of which he leaves to his wife.

Under those circumstances—and assuming he dies before she does—the $100,000 would have boosted the Federal estate tax in his estate by at least $12,700!

And that isn't all. In order for Mr. Brown to keep the tax in his own estate at a minimum, he must leave about half his estate to Mrs. Brown in such a way that it becomes taxable when she dies. The figuring here becomes a little involved, but it is accurate to say that an extra $100,000 in Mr. Brown's estate might increase the tax at Mrs. Brown's death by another $12,700.

$25,400 more in Federal estate tax, then, might have been payable if Mr. Brown had not made the gifts during his lifetime. Compare that with the $540 gift tax!

GIFTS BY UNMARRIED PERSONS

Gifts save tax only if they are final and irrevocable. A revocable gift doesn't keep the property from being taxed at the donor's death.

Why should an unmarried person part forever with a considerable portion of his property? He might save tax, yes. But the tax saving would never make up for the loss of the property. Generally, therefore, the maxim that it's cheaper to pay gift tax than estate tax is of interest only to married persons, who have wives, children, or grandchildren. Large, irrevocable gifts by married persons are natural; but, as a general rule, such gifts by unmarried persons are unnatural.

There are two marked exceptions to this general rule: gifts (1) by widows and (2) by widowers, to their children and grandchildren.

"But do unmarried persons obtain the same tax advantage in making gifts?" it may be asked. "Their gift tax would be high, since it isn't lowered by marital deductions and the split-gifts principle."

Their estate tax is high too—very high, in some cases, with no marital deduction available. Of course, this assumes the widow or widower does not remarry. If there should be a re-marriage, the estate tax marital deduction would be allowed for property left to the new wife or husband, just as in the case of other married couples.

Barring remarriage, however, the easiest way for a wealthy widow or widower to reduce an excessively high estate tax is to give property, irrevocably, to children or grandchildren.

EXAMPLE: *Mrs. Smith owns property valued at $500,000. Most of this came to her from the estate of her deceased husband. It gave his estate a large marital deduction, but it may boost the estate tax payable by Mrs. Smith's estate. The Federal tax alone on her $500,000 would be $116,500. State inheritance taxes and the expenses of settling her estate would be wholly in addition.*

Mrs. Smith has a son who needs capital in his business. Mrs. Smith is interested in helping him out and in avoiding the responsibilities connected with managing so much property. She is also *anxious to bring her income taxes down. So she gives her son $200,000.*

Mrs. Smith pays a gift tax of $30,600 on the gift. With that tax and the $200,000 gift taken away, only $269,400 of her $500,000 remains. The Federal estate tax on that $269,400 at her death will be $50,654.

(We are assuming the $200,000 gift is not considered made in contemplation of death. Mrs. Smith was not just trying to save estate tax. In any case, her motives wouldn't matter if she lived at least three years after making the gift.)

Although Mrs. Smith, in giving her son $200,000, was not primarily interested in estate tax savings, she is pleased to learn that she has saved more than $35,000 in tax. Here are the figures:

Estate tax if she had made no gift		$116,500
Her actual taxes:		
Gift tax	$30,600	
Estate tax	50,654	81,254
Saving		$ 35,246

In addition, there are considerable savings of State inheritance taxes and estate settlement costs. Her income taxes are lower too, because the income produced by the $200,000 is now taxed to the son.

Tax savings like Mrs. Smith's are available to more people now than in past years. The reason for this lies in the marital-deduction principle that was introduced into the Federal tax system in 1948. Formerly a wealthy man usually found it advantageous to tie all his property up in trust for his widow, in a trust that would eliminate any tax at the widow's death. But nowadays a husband, in order to obtain a marital deduction for his estate, usually leaves a considerable part of his property outright to his widow. This saves tax in his estate but may leave quite an estate tax to be paid when the widow dies. Gifts by the widow during her lifetime—if not primarily motivated by contemplation of death—can substantially lower that tax.

Note, however, that a husband can obtain a marital deduction for his estate by leaving property for the widow in trust —as well as outright—provided he gives the widow a certain degree of control over the principal. For instance, a trust set up by the husband's will would qualify for the deduction if it gave the widow the income for life plus the right to name the persons to receive the principal at her death (see Chapter 4).

Property in a trust like that will be taxed at the widow's death, if she still has the control over the principal when she dies. Can she give up that control and thereby save tax? It may be rather difficult under the law of her State to do so. Also, it may be difficult for her to offer any good reason for doing so other than the aim to save estate tax; in which case any saving of tax might be canceled out, if she should die within three years after giving up the control, by the charge that she was motivated by contemplation of death.

This possible tax problem of the widow's is something the husband should consider when making his will. Perhaps it will not seriously concern any but the wealthiest of married couples. But it is advisable for everyone to look ahead. Estate tax exemptions may be lower, and rates may be higher, when your widow dies. In having your will drawn to obtain a marital deduction in your estate, ask your lawyer if your plans will create tax problems for your widow.

16

Save Tax by Gifts to Charities

> ► *An income tax deduction for a "contribution" that is often overlooked. Big tax savings from small trust. Making sure the charity will receive gift. Charitable gifts via life insurance. Gifts to charity by will. Combined gifts by will to wife and charity.*

Everybody knows how charitable gifts help to reduce income tax. The most common deduction on Federal income tax returns is the one for contributions to charitable, religious, educational, etc., organizations.

Even so, some persons overlook large deductions for contributions.

EXAMPLE: *In 1955 Mr. Black sets up an irrevocable trust for his daughter. The income is to be paid to the daughter as long as she lives. At her death, according to the trust agreement, the trust is to end and the principal is to be paid to the ABC Hospital.*

When Mr. Black files his 1955 income tax return, he is quite likely to overlook the fact that, in putting property into this trust, he has made a contribution to the hospital.

The contribution isn't considered to be the full amount he has put in the trust. It must be discounted for the delay

236

that will occur before the hospital will get it. The amount of that discount depends on the daughter's age.

EXAMPLE: *Let's say Mr. Black put $30,000 in the trust in 1955. The daughter is thirty-seven years old.*

From the table on page 270 you will see that $1 payable after a person now aged thirty-seven dies is now considered to be worth only about 34¢.

Therefore, $30,000 × 34¢, or $10,200, is the amount of Mr. Black's contribution in 1955. He can deduct that $10,200 on his 1955 income tax return, except that he must keep in mind that his total contributions deduction must not be more than 20 per cent or 30 per cent in some cases of his adjusted gross income.

When Mr. Black hears about this privilege he says: "There must be some mistake. I've been told that the $10,200 figure is my *gift* tax deduction."

It's his income tax deduction too.

And that isn't all. Just in case the tax authorities should give special attention to that trust at Mr. Black's death and charge that he had created it in contemplation of death (as they might if he should die within three years of the gift), Mr. Black's estate would get an *estate* tax deduction for the same gift to the hospital. But at that time, of course, the daughter would be older, and the actual receipt of the money by the hospital wouldn't be so far in the future; so it would be discounted less, for estate tax purposes, and might be considerably more than $10,200.*

---

* All tax deductions—income, estate, and gift—connected with Mr. Black's trust might be lost if the trust engaged in "prohibited trans-

BIG TAX SAVINGS FROM SMALL TRUST

Here is a summary of the tax effect of Mr. Black's $30,000 trust: (Assume Mr. Black is unmarried, his income is about $20,000 a year, and he has an estate of about $200,000.)

$2,000 saved in Mr. Black's 1955 income tax. His contribution to the hospital is considered to be $10,200. But he can deduct only $4,000 of it because that's the top limit (20 per cent of his adjusted gross income)* on his contributions deduction. A $4,000 deduction reduces his 1955 tax by approximately $2,000, inasmuch as his highest tax rate is in the neighborhood of 50 per cent.

$750 saved in Mr. Black's income taxes each year after 1955. The $30,000 that he puts into the trust produces an income of about $1,500 a year. Mr. Black was taxed for that $1,500 before making the trust, but afterward his daughter is. With Mr. Black's income being taxed as high as 50 per cent, $1,500 less income means $750 less tax.

$8,520 saved in the Federal estate tax on Mr. Black's estate. The Federal tax on a $200,000 estate is $31,500. On a $170,-000 estate it is $8,250 less. By creating the trust, Mr. Black reduced his taxable estate from $200,000 to $170,000. (This assumes the trust was not created in contemplation of death. If it should be so considered, this estate tax saving would be

---

actions." See "Watch Out for 'Prohibited Transactions,'" page 126. The payment of income to Mr. Black's daughter would not be a prohibited transaction.

* The 1954 tax law raised the top limit from 20% of adjusted gross income to 30%, provided at least 10% of adjusted gross income is given to schools, hospitals, or churches. But notice that, as to the extra 10%, the gift must be made "to" the organization; a gift "for the use of" the organization—as, in trust—would not qualify. It is assumed, therefore, that Mr. Black's limit remains at 20%.

THE CAPITAL GAINS TAX CAN BE ELIMINATED TOO

Here is still another tax advantage in connection with a trust that eventually goes to charity:

In the example of Mr. Black's $30,000 trust, assume that the $30,000 consists of stocks worth that much which Mr. Black bought long ago for $10,000. If he were to sell those stocks he would have a $20,000 gain to report on his income tax return. But if the trust sells them, the gain is tax exempt. *Reason:* the gain is considered permanently set aside for the charity.

---

less, the exact amount depending on the age of the daughter at Mr. Black's death.)

No gift tax payable. Mr. Black, as we say, is considered to give $10,200 to the hospital upon putting the $30,000 into the trust. There's no gift tax on that gift, because gifts to charities are exempt. The rest of the $30,000—$19,800—is considered to be a gift to the daughter. It is looked upon as the value of her right to receive the income from $30,000 during her life. Gifts like that are subject to gift tax, all right, but Mr. Black's exemptions eliminate the tax. First, there is his $3,000 annual exclusion, bringing the gift down to $16,800. Then Mr. Black wipes that out with his $30,000 lifetime exemption. (See Chapter 7 on these exemptions.)

MAKING SURE THE CHARITY WILL RECEIVE THE MONEY

A useful provision in many trust agreements allows the trustee to pay some of the principal, in addition to the income, to the beneficiary in case the beneficiary has big medical bills or for some other reason needs extra money.

Be careful, though, about putting that kind of a provision

in a trust that eventually goes to charity. It may make it impossible for anyone to say how much the charity will get, or that it will get anything at all. Under those circumstances the tax advantages are lost.

Discuss this question with your tax adviser.

USING LIFE INSURANCE TO MAKE CHARITABLE GIFTS

Suppose you want to create a scholarship at a certain university or build a library for your home town. That takes a lot of money all at once. Piecemeal gifts wouldn't do.

You could save the money and leave it for the charitable purpose under your will.

A better way, though, might be like this: you take out insurance on your life for the amount needed and then assign the policy, irrevocably, to a trustee. You instruct the trustee, in a trust agreement, to devote the insurance proceeds at your death to the charitable purpose. Then you pay the premiums on the insurance—*and get contribution deductions on your income tax return for doing so.* In this case you do not need to discount the premium amounts; you can consider them contributions in full.

(If you merely saved this money, putting it in a fund of your own with the idea of leaving it to the charity in your will, you would of course get no income tax deductions.)

Then at your death the insurance proceeds would escape the estate tax.

GIFTS TO CHARITY BY WILL

If you leave, say, a $5,000 legacy to a charity, your estate gets a $5,000 deduction for estate tax. This deduction, like all other estate tax deductions, comes off the top of the estate; that is, it removes $5,000 of your property from the impact of the highest rates of tax on your estate. The net cost to your estate, therefore, of a charitable gift may be considerably less than the amount of the gift.

"I should like to leave some of my estate to a charity," a man says to his lawyer, "but I can't afford to. My dependents are going to need every cent of the income from my money while they live."

A man in this situation may find that he can leave a *bigger* income to his dependents if he does leave money to charities.

Here is the reason. If he leaves everything outright to the dependents, the estate tax must be paid and it is only what is left that goes to the dependents. That estate tax can be reduced or eliminated—leaving a bigger sum to support the dependents—by gifts of "remainder interests" to charities.

For example, Mr. White has an estate of $200,000. If he should leave all of that outright to his two invalid sisters, the Federal estate tax would be $31,500 and only $168,500 would remain for the sisters.

Instead, he leaves his money to the sisters in trust. They are to receive all the income from the trusts while they live, and at their deaths the principal is to be turned over to certain charities. These delayed gifts, or remainder interests in the trusts, may give Mr. White's estate such a big deduction for estate tax that there is no tax payable at all. Thus, the full $200,000—instead of just $168,500—can be invested for the sisters.

GIFTS BY WILL TO WIFE AND CHARITIES

A more typical situation than Mr. White's is Mr. Green's. He has a wife, no children. His property is valued at $300,-000. By leaving half of this to Mrs. Green in such a way as to give his estate a marital deduction, he can bring the Federal tax on his estate down to $17,500 (see Chapter 4).

But maybe he can even wipe out that $17,500!

He finds that it can be done like this:

The other half of his estate—the half that is not to give his estate a marital deduction—he leaves in trust for Mrs. Green. The income is to be paid to her as long as she lives, and at her death the principal is to be distributed among certain charities.

Here is the way his estate tax will be figured:

His estate, after debts and expenses are paid	$300,000
Less the marital deduction	150,000
	$150,000
Less a charitable deduction (This is for the discounted value at Mr. Green's death of the $150,000 trust principal that will eventually be paid to the charities. It is assumed Mrs. Green is 65 years old when Mr. Green dies)	100,000
	$ 50,000

The $50,000 is less than the estate's $60,000 exemption, so there is no tax.

The point to keep in mind here is that the charitable deduction is in addition to the marital deduction. The latter —the marital deduction—can be up to half the adjusted gross estate. In figuring the adjusted gross estate you do not take off anything for gifts to charities, so the top limit on the marital deduction is unaffected by such gifts.

In combination, the marital and charitable deductions sometimes produce astonishing tax savings. In New York, for instance, a man with ten million dollars can eliminate both the Federal and New York taxes on his estate. All he has to do is leave half his property to his wife and half to a charity, the charitable bequest being outright. Each of the two deductions would be for five million dollars, leaving a net taxable estate of zero.

17

Don't Let "Tax Lightning" Strike Your Business

► *How a business was lost. Creating liquidity in the estate. Bringing sons and daughters in as partners. Selling a business for an annuity. Pre-arranged sale to business associate. Prearranged sale to key employee. Prearranged sale to the company itself ("stock retirement plan"). How the 1950, 1951, and 1954 tax laws give a boost to stock retirement plans.*

HOW A BUSINESS WAS LOST

Look at what happened to this businessman's estate:

The businessman—Mr. X, we'll call him—owned a small but prosperous business. He judged it would be worth about $80,000—at the most, $100,000—if he were to die. He wanted his son to own this business someday. So he had made a will leaving all his estate, including the business, in trust. Mrs. X would receive the income for life, with the trust to end at her death and the principal turned over to the son.

Apart from the business, Mr. X owned his home and a few security investments. He also carried $75,000 life insurance payable to Mrs. X.

This estate plan seemed sound enough. The $75,000 of insurance would entitle his estate to a $75,000 marital deduction, leaving little tax to pay. If the estate should be a little short of cash to pay the tax, then Mrs. X could contribute some of the insurance money for that purpose. Mrs. X would have an adequate income, for the business produced a good profit, year in and year out.

And the son would eventually have the business. This was an important point to Mr. X.

But when Mr. X died, the business was valued for estate-tax purposes at $270,600! Here is the arithmetic:

Value of net assets, not including good will		$ 80,000
Average net earnings during five years preceding death	$35,000	
Earnings attributable to tangible assets (8 per cent of $80,000)	6,400	
Earnings attributable to good will	$28,600	
Value of good will ($28,600 capitalized at 15 per cent)		$190,600
Total value of business, including good will		$270,600

That made a valuation of Mr. X's whole estate of nearly $400,000. The Federal tax came to $65,000, and the State tax was several thousand dollars in addition. *Result:* the business had to be sold, at a sacrifice price, to raise the cash. The life insurance plus the few investments in the estate were far from enough to pay taxes, expenses, and debts.

PAY THE TAX IN INSTALLMENTS?

Mr. X died before September, 1958, when the 1958 law added a valuable relief provision to the Federal estate tax. It is now possible for some or all of the tax on a business owner's estate, in certain circumstances to be paid in as many as 10 equal annual installments with 4% interest.

THE GOVERNMENT'S "FORMULA" FOR VALUING BUSINESSES

Many years ago the Bureau of Internal Revenue issued a ruling on the valuation of businesses for income tax purposes. This ruling, containing a formula for valuing good will, has often been advanced by the government in connection with estate and gift tax valuations. The formula, or variations of it, has been approved by the courts in a number of instances, although it is and always has been merely a general guide to valuation, and is not to be applied in every case. Here are the important parts:

The . . . method . . . is to allow out of average earnings over a period of years . . . preferably not less than five years, a return of 10% upon the average tangible assets for the period. The surplus earnings will then be the average amount available for return upon the value of the intangible assets, and it is the opinion of the Committee that this return should be capitalized upon the basis of not more than five years' purchase— that is to say, five times the amount available as return from intangibles should be the value of the intangibles.

The foregoing is intended to apply particularly to businesses put out of existence by the prohibition law, but will be equally applicable so far as the . . . formula is concerned, to other businesses of a more or less hazardous nature. In the case, however, of valuation of good will of a business which consists of the manufacture or sale of standard articles of every-day necessity not subject to violent fluctuations and where the hazard is not so great, the Committee is of the opinion that the figure for determination of the return on tangible assets might be reduced from 10 to 8 or 9 per cent, and that the percentage for capitalization of the return upon intangibles might be reduced from 20 to 15 per cent. [A.R.M. 34, CB-2, p. 31]

Perhaps your estate will qualify for the installment-payment privilege. The requirements are technical, and your lawyer's advice should be sought on the question. Yet the privilege, even if available, might be thought of as cushioning rather than lightening the tax. Interest at 4% must be paid on the postponed installments. The estate, burdened with tax plus interest, may still be compelled to sell or liquidate the business interest under unfavorable conditions.

For many business owners, therefore, the liquidity problem remains. Below are several plans that are being followed today to meet this problem.

CREATING LIQUIDITY IN THE ESTATE

The simplest plan is for the business owner to estimate with care the amount of cash his estate will need, then to make sure that his estate will have that much cash.

The largest cash outlay by his estate will, in many cases, be the Federal estate tax. That will depend upon the valuation placed on his business, of course. So, in estimating the tax on your estate, use a value for your business that errs, if at all, on the high side. Can it be said that your business will still possess valuable good will if you were out of the picture? If the answer is yes, compute a value for your business by using the government's formula (see page 246). Perhaps that will double or triple the value as shown by the books. Nevertheless, in estimating your tax, you are risking an underestimate if you do not take into account the fact that the tax authorities will aggressively collect as large a tax as they can.

TAKING CASH OUT OF A BUSINESS TO PAY ESTATE TAX

Instead of *selling* a business to raise cash for taxes, the executor sometimes *liquidates* the business.

The complete liquidation of a business may result in a tremendous loss of values, perhaps even a larger loss than would result from a sale. But a partial liquidation may be practical. The business may have cash or marketable securities to spare, so that enough could be withdrawn to pay the estate and inheritance taxes in the estate without affecting the earning power of the business.

If the business is incorporated, would not the withdrawal of cash be considered a dividend and taxed to the estate at the ordinary rates of tax? Until the enactment of the Revenue Act of 1950, such a threat was always present if the company had an accumulation of earned surplus. But a relief provision of the 1950 act puts an end to the danger of a dividends tax, if certain conditions are met. See "How the 1950, 1951, and 1954 Tax Laws give a Boost to Stock Retirement Plans," page 261, for full details.

As for ways and means of putting more liquid assets into your estate, life insurance may be the solution. If you are insurable, consider taking out more insurance.

Should this insurance be payable to your estate (to your executor, that is)? Perhaps that would be the safest course; but it would result in the inclusion of the insurance in your estate for estate tax purposes. Possibly, if you make the policies payable to a member of your family, and if you assign the policies to this beneficiary, you can be satisfied that the beneficiary will use the insurance proceeds to pay the tax on your estate; and in this latter situation the insurance would not necessarily be taxed as a part of your estate. It is an arrangement, however, that you should discuss with your lawyer beforehand. If the beneficiary of the insurance should decline to pay the tax, then your estate might be left in a decidedly unliquid position.

What other assets do you own? Have you a costly residence—an asset that might be fully taxed yet which might not be readily salable to help pay the tax? Your estate might be much better prepared for a heavy tax blow if you did not have your money tied up in that or any other kind of real estate.

Liquidity is essential. Your estate may not be able to borrow money to pay taxes. The executor usually has no other course available than to dip down into the estate assets for the cash. Don't compel him to throw your hard-to-sell business on the market to raise the needed money.

BRINGING SONS AND DAUGHTERS INTO THE BUSINESS

If a man keeps his entire interest in a business until he dies, that interest will be taxed in his estate.

But if he gives his son, for instance, half of the interest, then only the remaining half ordinarily will be taxed.

For reasons having nothing to do with estate taxes, it is perfectly natural for a man to bring his children into his business as partners or as owners of some of the corporate stock, while he is still living. The children gradually take over the active management, allowing their father to retire. At his death they inherit the remaining interest, with no abrupt change-over in the policies of the business. A gradual transfer like this of the ownership of a business is good for the business and it's good for the business owner.

It also is likely to solve his estate tax problem. For, with only a fraction of the business left to be taxed when he dies, the tax may be much less than if the whole business were taxed.

Under certain conditions, the bringing in of a son or daughter as a partner might be regarded as a transfer in contemplation of death (but there is no danger of this if the business owner lives at least three years afterward). In that case the estate tax advantage could be wiped out. However, there are so many other good reasons for such a transfer of ownership that contemplation of death is most unlikely to be regarded as the dominant motive. It is a matter that you should discuss with your lawyer before actually taking any steps to share the business with your children.

As a matter of fact, it may be doubtful, where the business is unincorporated, that any gift to the new partners occurs. They acquire shares in the business, yes. But they may contribute their services, and they may become personally liable for any losses of the business. Therefore, it may be argued, their father gives them nothing in bringing them in as partners. And if that argument is sustained, the shares in the business transferred to them could not possibly be taxed in the parent's estate, nor would the parent be faced with a gift tax. (See Chapter 8 on this question of whether a gift occurs.)

SELLING A BUSINESS FOR AN ANNUITY

Suppose the owner of a business wants to have one or more of his adult children take over the entire business. But he can't afford to give it to them. If he did that, he would be left with little or no income.

Or, suppose he wants a son to have just a 30, 40, or 50 per cent interest in the business. But he can't give away even that much. It would make too serious an inroad upon his income.

"There ought to be some practical way to pass the business on to my children," the business owner says to his attorney. "They know the business from top to bottom. They have the inclination and the ability to run it. If they had the incentive that goes with ownership, they'd make the company more profitable than ever."

"Sell it to them," the attorney suggests. "Have them pay you in the form of an annuity."

"For example," the attorney continues, "let's say the interest you want to part with is worth $80,000. If you went to an insurance company with $80,000 cash you could, at your present age, buy an annuity paying you about $5,000 a year for the rest of your life. All right, have the children agree to pay you $5,000 a year, and in return you let them have the business interest."

The business owner objects to annuities. "Nothing will be left when I die," he says. But the attorney points out that the transaction would be between the business owner and his children, to whom he planned to leave his property anyway. If, from any imaginable standpoint, the business owner should appear to be the loser, his children must be the gainers. His property would not evaporate into thin air.

Moreover, the business owner's very objection that "nothing would be left" at his death brings up the estate tax saving: *$80,000 of his property would escape estate tax at his death*.

He would no longer own the business interest, nor would he have—at his death—anything in place of it. Therefore his taxable estate would be reduced by $80,000.

What about a gift tax?

"No," the attorney says, "there's no gift tax to pay. If you get a fair price for your business interest—if your children agree to pay a big enough annuity—you have not made a gift to anyone."

So far, the arrangement of selling a business interest to a member of the family in return for a life annuity may appear to offer nothing but advantages. However, there are disadvantages too. The disadvantages will in many cases outweigh the advantages, so the arrangement is far from being the basis of a model estate plan for the businessman. It is merely one possible solution to his problems. This solution ought to be considered along with other arrangements that have worked out satisfactorily—the more usual ones are outlined in this chapter—and a choice should be made of the arrangement that best fits the particular business and family situation.

The biggest drawback to a sale-for-an-annuity arrangement is likely to be the income tax result. It is, after all, a sale of the business or of a part of the business. The sale takes place during the business owner's lifetime. Therefore, if the business owner cannot show a substantial cost basis for the interest he disposes of, he will have a large gain and, possibly, a large tax.

The entire gain may not be taxable in the year the arrangement is entered into. Perhaps a taxable gain on the "sale" is not reportable until certain portions of the annuity payments have wiped out your cost of the business interest. (See, as to income tax, Revenue Ruling 239, IRB 1953-23.)

These income tax results in detail are beyond the scope of this book. If you feel that a sale-for-an-annuity would be the best thing for your business, ask your tax adviser to make calculations of your income and of your income tax on an after-sale state of facts. Compare the estimated net amount of income, as reduced by the tax, with your present income from the business interest, similarly reduced by income tax. Then take into consideration the very substantial estate tax saving you would probably obtain as a result of the sale and see if, on balance, the arrangement as a whole is advantageous from a tax viewpoint.

In making these comparisons, however, remember that the estate tax saving may be worth more than the mere number of dollars indicates. Without the reduction in estate tax, your executors may be compelled to sell or liquidate the business —at a sacrifice of values—to raise money to pay the tax. Any plan or arrangement that lessens the danger of such a forced sale or liquidation may be advantageous even though, on a direct comparison of taxes, it appears uneconomical.

PREARRANGED SALE TO BUSINESS ASSOCIATE

A "business-purchase agreement" is the ideal solution to the business owner's tax problems in many situations. Here is a typical arrangement of this nature:

Smith and Jones each own half the stock of a small company. They get along well together. But neither of them feels he would like to be in business with any members of his associate's family.

So Smith and Jones enter into an agreement. Smith agrees that, if he dies first, his estate will sell his stock to Jones at a certain price, and Jones agrees to buy it from Smith's estate. Conversely, Jones binds his estate to sell to Smith if Smith should be the survivor, and Smith agrees to buy from Jones's estate.

The agreed price can be a stated amount per share or it can be book value or based in some way on book value.

NO CAPITAL-GAINS TAX IN BUSINESS-PURCHASE ARRANGEMENTS

Many a business has been started on a shoestring. If the estate of one owner sells an interest—for a good price—to the surviving owner, won't the estate have to pay a large income tax on the gain?

No, because ordinarily there is no gain. The seller is the estate. The estate's cost is the market value at date of death. That market value is the same as the agreed-upon selling price, the Internal Revenue Service has ruled in a typical situation. So it doesn't matter how much the value of the business has increased since it was started.

This ruling is applicable whether the business is a corporation or a partnership.

To make sure the purchase money will be ready when needed, Jones takes out insurance on Smith's life and Smith takes out insurance on Jones's life. A trustee is named as beneficiary under the insurance. The trustee holds the stock.

When one of the owners dies the trustee collects the insurance proceeds, pays it to the estate of the one who has died, and gives all the stock to the survivor. That leaves the survivor owning the whole business, with no heirs of his deceased associate to harass him. The business continues on an even keel.

Now let's see what this arrangement does for the estate of the owner who dies first.

(1) The estate receives ample cash, almost immediately, as proceeds of sale of the business interest. A decidedly non-liquid asset—the business interest—is converted overnight into cash, with no hurried search for buyers and no sacrifice of values.

(2) The value of that business interest is "pegged" for estate tax purposes at the selling price. It has worked out that way, at least, in quite a number of instances. Ask your attorney if the valuation of your business for estate tax purposes cannot be nailed down, during your lifetime, by means of a business-purchase agreement.

One remaining point: The estate of the deceased businessman usually ends up owning some insurance on the life of the businessman who survived. What happens to that insurance? Well, the estate can surrender it for cash or sell it to the surviving businessman. There may be some loss of values involved in this insurance which turns out to be no longer necessary under the agreement; but the loss is likely to be small in relation to the benefits from the agreement.

PREARRANGED SALE TO ONE OR MORE KEY EMPLOYEES

If a man owns *all* of a business, can he hope to find anyone who will agree to buy the business from his estate?

Yes, very often. There may be a key employee—a man who has worked a long time for the business, who is capable of managing it, and who wants to own an interest in it. The owner can enter into an agreement with that employee like this:

> The owner binds his estate to sell an interest in the business to the employee at the owner's death. The employee, on his part, agrees to buy. As for a price, it can be stated in dollars and cents, or else it can be based on book value.

> The employee makes sure he will have the money when needed by taking out insurance on the owner's life.

The employee pays the insurance premiums with his own money. Ordinarily the employee will be able to take out and pay for only enough insurance to buy a fractional interest in the business, so this type of business-purchase arrangement may solve the businessman's estate problem only in part (unless a number of employees join together in the purchase).

However, a fractional sale of the business—30 per cent, for example—may be quite enough to bring ample cash into the estate for taxes, debts, and expenses. The rest of the business could be left under the businessman's will to his widow, children, or other dependents. Although the widow and children may be inexperienced in business affairs, this remaining interest in the business might be a suitable investment for them so long as the key man—now an employee-stockholder—is actively looking after the day-to-day operations of the business.

Whether the agreement covers all or, on the other hand, only a part of the business, the estate tax valuation of the interest covered is ordinarily pegged at the agreed price. Apparently the agreement would not peg the tax valuation of an interest not covered by the agreement.

CONTINGENCIES: It could be provided in the agreement that if the key employee should die before the business owner, the business owner should buy the insurance from the employee's estate. The business owner might need additional insurance anyway, so even if he should refund to the employee's estate the full amount of premiums paid so far, no real loss would be involved.

Likewise, if the key employee should quit his job during the business owner's lifetime, the business owner could buy up the policy. However, the employee probably wouldn't quit his job. One of the advantages of a business-purchase arrangement like this is that it creates incentive on the part of the business's most valuable employees.

Insurance that would be "picked up" by the business owner in this way would not cause a capital-gains tax when the business owner dies. There are situations where, if you buy an already existing policy, you do run into a gains tax when the insured person dies; but that rule doesn't apply to a policy *on your own life* that you buy from somebody.

PREARRANGED SALE TO THE COMPANY (STOCK RETIREMENT PLAN)

One drawback to the business-purchase arrangements outlined so far is that they usually must be financed out of salaries.

For instance, take the case of Jones and Smith, who each owned half the stock of a corporation. Jones took out insurance on Smith's life, and Smith took out insurance on Jones's life. The premiums would be fairly large amounts each year. Could Jones and Smith afford those premiums?

They could if their salaries were quite large. However, the income tax authorities watch the salaries that owners of small, closely held companies vote for themselves. If the salary of a stockholder-employee is unreasonably large, the Revenue agents will not allow the company to take an income tax deduction for the full amount paid.

So, in a situation like Smith's and Jones's, the business owners may not be able to afford premiums on any new insurance. And they may already be paying themselves all the salary their company can deduct on its tax returns. How can they arrange for the sale of their stock by their estates?

They should ask their attorney to study the problem. One possible solution might be a stock retirement plan. Under

HOW TO SELL ALL THE COMMON STOCK TO KEY EMPLOYEES

If a man who owns 100 per cent of a company's stock proposes a buy-and-sell agreement with key employees, he is likely to find that the employees can't afford to buy from his estate more than a fraction of his holdings—25 or 30 per cent, say.

Considering the effect on the liquidity of the business owner's estate, that may be enough stock to sell. For example, if a company's net worth is $200,000, the business owner's estate might obtain $50,000 cash from the employees under a buy-and-sell agreement. The estate would part with 25 per cent of its stock, leaving a controlling interest of 75 per cent to go outright to the widow or to be held in trust for her. The $50,000 cash, along with any other liquid assets in the estate, might be ample to pay taxes, debts, and expenses.

"But," it may be objected, "a buy-and-sell agreement like that would peg the estate tax valuation of only the 25 per cent interest. The government might add a good-will value to the remaining stock, boosting the estate tax sky-high."

The objection is valid. A buy-and-sell agreement could have little effect in determining the value of stock not subject to the agreement.

But here is a possible solution to the problem: issue preferred stock, and in this way bring within reach of the employees all the stock that might be considered to carry a good-will value.

EXAMPLE: *A man owns all the capital stock of a certain company. It has a book value of $200,000. Re-*

> *capitalizing, the company issues 1,500 shares of*
> *$100 par, 6 per cent preferred stock to the stock-*
> *holder. That leaves him owning preferred stock*
> *worth $150,000 and common stock worth*
> *$50,000.*
>
> *Then he enters into an agreement with key em-*
> *ployees under which they will buy from his*
> *estate all the common stock at book value.*

If the preferred stock is properly limited as to its share of earnings and its share of assets upon liquidation, it is diffi-cult to see how it could be valued for estate tax purposes at much above par. And the common stock could hardly be valued in excess of the price (book value) set by the agree-ment, provided the agreement bound both the estate and the employees and was entered into at arm's length.

"Wouldn't the business owner be taxed for a dividend upon receiving the distribution of preferred stock?" it may be asked.

No, the 1954 tax law provides, as a general rule, that no tax will be imposed on shareholders when stock dividends are distributed to them—and this is so whether or not any shareholder's proportionate interest in the company is changed by the distribution. If the stockholder turns around and sells some of his newly acquired preferred stock, or if the company redeems it, some or all of the proceeds might be taxed as ordinary income. Note, how-ever, that the business owner—or, rather, his estate—sells the *common* stock, not the preferred. So there appears to be no danger of a dividend tax in the arrangement.

this arrangement a stockholder enters into an agreement with the company. The stockholder binds his estate to sell, and the company agrees to buy, all or a part of the stock when the stockholder dies. The price might be stated as so many dollars, or it might be based on book value.

To finance the agreement the company could take out insurance on the stockholder's life. The company itself could be the beneficiary of the policies and would use the proceeds to buy the stock from the estate. The company would not be allowed tax deductions for the premiums paid, but on the other hand, the company would not have to pay any income tax by reason of receiving the insurance proceeds at the stockholder's death.

Obviously a sole stockholder would not agree to have his estate sell *all* his stock to his company, for there would be no one left to own the business; the transaction would be merely an awkward way of carrying out a complete liquidation. A sole stockholder could, however, arrange for a sale to the company of a part of his stock holdings.

Where there are two or more stockholders, the purchase by the company of all the shares held by a stockholder who dies has the same effect upon the control of the company as would a purchase by the surviving stockholders. In either case the surviving stockholders acquire the deceased stockholder's interest. And, if the company pays real value for the shares it acquires under a stock retirement plan, the intrinsic values of the interests of the other stockholders are unaffected.

EXAMPLE: *Mr. A and Mr. B each own half the stock of XYZ Co. The company's net worth is $500,000. Mr. A dies and his executors sell all his stock to the company for $250,000. That leaves Mr. B* *owning the company 100 per cent, just as if he had purchased Mr. A's stock. And the value of Mr. B's stock is $250,000, just as it was before the sale to the company took place.*

A stock retirement plan may be adversely affected by some State laws. Also, the possibility that the payment by the company may be taxed as a dividend must be looked into. Finally, the tax authorities might conceivably claim that the agreement is not sufficiently binding on the parties to peg the valuation of the stock for estate tax purposes. However, your attorney should advise you on these points. So far as the financing of the agreement is concerned—the taking out of insurance by the company on the life of someone who is largely responsible for the company's success—that is tried and tested. "Key-man insurance" has been in use for years and has saved many a small company from disaster. It would be a deserved aid to the business owner, faced as he sometimes is with a ruinous estate tax on his business, if he could under all conditions count on the effectiveness of a stock retirement plan.

HOW THE 1950, 1951, AND 1954 TAX LAWS GIVE A BOOST TO STOCK RETIREMENT PLANS

A difficulty connected with stock retirement plans has been partially ironed out by a relief provision contained in the Internal Revenue Code of 1954 (section 303).

Under this provision—it was first introduced in 1950, and amended in 1951 and 1954—the businessman's estate can avoid all danger that payments to it by a corporation in redemption of its stock will be taxed as a dividend.

To illustrate, suppose an estate holds most of the stock of a small but prosperous company. The business owner, while living, had entered into an agreement with the company under which the company was to buy—and the business owner's estate was to sell—30 per cent of his stock at book value existing at date of death.

But the company has a huge earned surplus. Would not the Federal tax authorities say that this "sale" was just a devious way of paying a dividend to a stockholder?

The tax authorities might have taken that stand prior to September 23, 1950, the effective date of the 1950 Act. But as to stock "cashed in" like this now, the payment by the company will NOT be taxed as a dividend if:

(1) the stock was a part of someone's estate for Federal estate tax purposes; and

(2) the payment by the company takes place within (A) the period of the statute of limitations for the assessment of the Federal estate tax (such period to be determined without the application of certain sections of the tax law dealing with suspensions), or within ninety days after the expiration of that period, or (B) within sixty days after a decision of the Tax Court concerning the estate tax liability has become final; and

(3) the payment for the stock does not exceed the estate and inheritance taxes (including interest) on the estate, plus the amount of funeral and administration expenses allowable as estate tax deductions; and

(4) the value of the company's stock included in the estate for tax purposes is more than 35 per cent of the gross estate or 50 per cent of the net, or "taxable," estate.

Stock of two or more companies can be treated as that of one company for the percentage tests under (4), above, if more than 75 per cent in value of the outstanding stock of each company is included in the estate for estate tax purposes.

There are several points to be noted about this relief provision that may not at first be apparent.

First, condition (4) does not require that the value of the stock redeemed be more than 50 per cent of the net estate or 35 per cent of the gross estate. It requires only that the value of all the stock of that particular company included in the estate be over one of those percentages. Thus, if the estate holds $150,000 stock of a certain company, and if that amounts to more than 35 per cent of the gross estate or 50 per cent of the net estate, then all or any part of the $150,-000 (up to the amount of taxes and expenses) could be redeemed under the new relief provision.

Second, a Senate Finance Committee Report says:

> The [new provision] is applicable if the redeemed stock is includible in the decedent's gross estate, whether or not the stock is owned by the decedent at the time of his death and whether or not the redemption is from the estate of the decedent. For example, the [new provision] is applicable to the redemption of stock includible in the decedent's gross estate which the decedent had transferred in contemplation of death. The [new provision] is also applicable to the redemption of stock includible in the decedent's estate if such stock was distributed by the estate prior to the redemption. The [new provision], however, is not applicable to the redemption of stock from a purchaser for value thereof, even though such stock was includible in a decedent's gross estate.

Thus, a legatee could take advantage of the new provision, cashing in stock after receiving it from the executor. Under certain conditions, however, it seems possible that a legatee could be barred as a "purchaser for value." Suppose a will provides a general legacy of $100,000; and the executor, instead of paying $100,000 in cash, gives the legatee $100,000 worth of stock. Income tax cases have held the legatee "purchases" the stock from the estate.

Third, there doesn't seem to be any requirement that the proceeds of redemption be used to pay taxes. Suppose an estate has plenty of cash. Could it not cash in stock of a family corporation nevertheless, taking advantage of this singular opportunity to draw down surplus from the company free of income tax?

Fourth, resort to the new provision is unnecessary if *all* the stock owned by a stockholder is cashed in.* The Regulations have exempted such a transaction for a long time. It is only where *some* of a stockholder's shares are cashed in that the new provision is important.

The relatively new stock redemption provision will be helpful to the estates of thousands of businessmen. It is one of the best solutions in sight to the liquidity problem. But the beneficial effects of this new provision may be completely denied to a business owner's estate unless he, while living, assures himself with regard to the two following questions:

(1) *Will the company be agreeable to buying his stock?*

(2) *Will the company itself be in a liquid position?*

A stock retirement plan, entered into between the businessman and his company, may provide the most satisfactory answers to both questions.

---

* *But be careful here. Stock held by others is sometimes "attributed" to a stockholder, so he does not necessarily get rid of all his stock by cashing in all that stands in his name.*

Part Five

DATA TO HELP YOU

The Federal Estate Tax Rates

TAXABLE ESTATE (BEFORE DEDUCTING THE $60,000 EXEMPTION)	GROSS TAX		MAXIMUM CREDIT FOR STATE INHERITANCE OR ESTATE TAXES		NET TAX	
	TAX	RATE ON NEXT BRACKET		RATE ON NEXT BRACKET	TAX	RATE ON NEXT BRACKET
$ 60,000	$ ..	3%	$ ..	..	$ ..	3%
65,000	150	7			150	7
70,000	500	11			500	11
80,000	1,600	14			1,600	14
90,000	3,000	18			3,000	18
100,000	4,800	22	..	0.8	4,800	21.2
110,000	7,000	25	80	0.8	6,920	24.2
120,000	9,500	28	160	0.8	9,340	27.2
150,000	17,900	28	400	1.6	17,500	26.4
160,000	20,700	30	560	1.6	20,140	28.4
200,000	32,700	30	1,200	2.4	31,500	27.6
300,000	62,700	30	3,600	3.2	59,100	26.8
310,000	65,700	32	3,920	3.2	61,780	28.8
500,000	126,500	32	10,000	4.0	116,500	28
560,000	145,700	35	12,400	4.0	133,300	31
700,000	194,700	35	18,000	4.8	176,700	30.2
810,000	233,200	37	23,280	4.8	209,920	32.2
900,000	266,500	37	27,600	5.6	238,900	31.4
1,060,000	325,700	39	36,560	5.6	289,140	33.4
1,100,000	341,300	39	38,800	6.4	302,500	32.6
1,310,000	423,200	42	52,240	6.4	370,960	35.6
1,560,000	528,200	45	68,240	6.4	459,960	38.6
1,600,000	546,200	45	70,800	7.2	475,400	37.8
2,060,000	753,200	49	103,920	7.2	649,280	41.8
2,100,000	772,800	49	106,800	8.0	666,000	41

TAXABLE ESTATE (BEFORE DEDUCTING THE $60,000 EXEMPTION)	GROSS TAX		MAXIMUM CREDIT FOR STATE INHERI- TANCE OR ESTATE TAXES		NET TAX	
	TAX	RATE ON NEXT BRACKET	TAX	RATE ON NEXT BRACKET	TAX	RATE ON NEXT BRACKET
$ 2,560,000	$ 998,200	53%	$ 143,600	8.0%	$ 854,600	45 %
2,600,000	1,019,400	53	146,800	8.8	873,600	44.2
3,060,000	1,263,200	56	187,280	8.8	1,075,920	47.2
3,100,000	1,285,600	56	190,800	9.6	1,094,800	46.4
3,560,000	1,543,200	59	234,960	9.6	1,308,240	49.4
3,600,000	1,566,800	59	238,800	10.4	1,328,000	48.6
4,060,000	1,838,200	63	286,640	10.4	1,551,560	52.6
4,100,000	1,863,400	63	290,800	11.2	1,572,600	51.8
5,060,000	2,468,200	67	398,320	11.2	2,069,880	55.8
5,100,000	2,495,000	67	402,800	12.0	2,092,200	55
6,060,000	3,138,200	70	518,000	12.0	2,620,200	58
6,100,000	3,166,200	70	522,800	12.8	2,643,400	57.2
7,060,000	3,838,200	73	645,680	12.8	3,192,520	60.2
7,100,000	3,867,400	73	650,800	13.6	3,216,600	59.4
8,060,000	4,568,200	76	781,360	13.6	3,786,840	62.4
8,100,000	4,598,600	76	786,800	14.4	3,811,800	61.6
9,100,000	5,358,600	76	930,800	15.2	4,427,800	60.8
10,060,000	6,088,200	77	1,076,720	15.2	5,011,480	61.8
10,100,000	6,119,000	77	1,082,800	16.0	5,036,200	61

EXAMPLE:

Gross estate		$480,000
Less—		
Debts and expenses	$ 80,000	
Marital deduction	200,000	280,000
Taxable estate, before deducting the $60,000 exemption		$200,000
Gross Federal tax, from table above		$ 32,700
State inheritance tax paid ($11,050, but only $1,200 allowed as credit against Federal tax)		1,200
Net Federal tax		$ 31,500

The Federal Gift Tax Rates

Applicable to gifts during 1942 and later years.

AMOUNT OF GIFT (BEFORE DEDUCTING THE $30,000 LIFETIME EXEMPTION AND THE $3,000 ANNUAL EXCLUSION)	TAX	RATE ON NEXT BRACKET
$ 33,000	$ –0–	2¼%
38,000	112.50	5¼
43,000	375	8¼
53,000	1,200	10½
63,000	2,250	13½
73,000	3,600	16½
83,000	5,250	18¾
93,000	7,125	21
133,000	15,525	22½
283,000	49,275	24
533,000	109,275	26¼
783,000	174,900	27¾
1,033,000	244,275	29¼
1,283,000	317,400	31½
1,533,000	396,150	33¾
2,033,000	564,900	36¾
2,533,000	748,650	39¾
3,033,000	947,400	42
3,533,000	1,157,400	44¼
4,033,000	1,378,650	47¼
5,033,000	1,851,150	50¼
6,033,000	2,353,650	52½
7,033,000	2,878,650	54¾
8,033,000	3,426,150	57
10,033,000	4,566,150	57¾

EXAMPLE:

Unmarried person makes $150,000 gift during 1955. Has made no other taxable gifts since June 6, 1932, when present gift tax system began.

Tax, from above table, on $133,000	$15,525
Tax on $17,000, @ 22½%	3,825
Total tax on gift	$19,350

Values of Life Estates and Remainders

TABLE I

TABLE, SINGLE LIFE, $3\frac{1}{2}$ PER CENT, SHOWING THE PRESENT WORTH OF
AN ANNUITY, OR A LIFE INTEREST, AND OF A REMAINDER INTEREST

1 AGE	2 ANNUITY	3 REMAINDER	1 AGE	2 ANNUITY	3 REMAINDER
0	23.9685	.16110	20	22.5179	.21187
1	24.9035	.12838	21	22.3438	.21797
2	24.8920	.12878	22	22.1646	.22424
3	24.8246	.13114	23	21.9801	.23070
4	24.7378	.13418	24	21.7902	.23734
5	24.6392	.13763	25	21.5950	.24418
6	24.5326	.14136	26	21.3942	.25120
7	24.4188	.14534	27	21.1878	.25843
8	24.2982	.14956	28	20.9759	.26584
9	24.1713	.15400	29	20.7581	.27347
10	24.0387	.15865	30	20.5345	.28129
11	23.9008	.16347	31	20.3052	.28932
12	23.7600	.16840	32	20.0699	.29755
13	23.6161	˙17344	33	19.8288	.30599
14	23.4693	.17857	34	19.5816	.31464
15	23.3194	.18382	35	19.3285	.32350
16	23.1665	.18917	36	19.0695	.33257
17	23.0103	.19464	37	18.8044	.34185
18	22.8511	.20021	38	18.5334	.35133
19	22.6870	.20596	39	18.2566	.36102

TABLE I—*Continued*

1 AGE	2 ANNUITY	3 REMAINDER	1 AGE	2 ANNUITY	3 REMAINDER
40	17.9738	.37092	73	6.8382	.76066
41	17.6853	.38101	74	6.5231	.77169
42	17.3911	.39131	75	6.2148	.78248
43	17.0913	.40180	76	5.9137	.79302
44	16.7860	.41249	77	5.6201	.80330
45	16.4754	.42336	78	5.3345	.81329
46	16.1596	.43441	79	5.0572	.82300
47	15.8388	.44564	80	4.7884	.83241
48	15.5133	.45703	81	4.5283	.84151
49	15.1831	.46859	82	4.2771	.85030
50	14.8486	.48030	83	4.0351	.85877
51	14.5101	.49215	84	3.8023	.86692
52	14.1678	.50413	85	3.5789	.87474
53	13.8221	.51623	86	3.3648	.88223
54	13.4734	.52843	87	3.1601	.88940
55	13.1218	.54074	88	2.9648	.89623
56	12.7679	.55312	89	2.7788	.90274
57	12.4120	.56558	90	2.6019	.90893
58	12.0546	.57809	91	2.4342	.91480
59	11.6960	.59064	92	2.2754	.92036
60	11.3369	.60321	93	2.1254	.92561
61	10.9776	.61578	94	1.9839	.93056
62	10.6186	.62835	95	1.8507	.93523
63	10.2604	.64089	96	1.7256	.93960
64	9.9036	.65337	97	1.6082	.94371
65	9.5486	.66580	98	1.4982	.94756
66	9.1960	.67814	99	1.3949	.95118
67	8.8464	.69038	100	1.2973	.95459
68	8.5001	.70250	101	1.2033	.95788
69	8.1578	.71448	102	1.1078	.96123
70	7.8200	.72630	103	.9973	.96509
71	7.4871	.73795	104	.8318	.97089
72	7.1597	.74941	105	.4831	.98309

TABLE II

TABLE SHOWING THE PRESENT WORTH AT $3\frac{1}{2}$ PER CENT OF AN ANNUITY
FOR A TERM-CERTAIN, AND OF A REMAINDER INTEREST POSTPONED FOR
A TERM-CERTAIN

1 NUMBER OF YEARS	2 ANNUITY	3 REMAINDER
1	0.9662	.966184
2	1.8997	.933511
3	2.8016	.901943
4	3.6731	.871442
5	4.5151	.841973
6	5.3286	.813501
7	6.1145	.785991
8	6.8740	.759412
9	7.6077	.733731
10	8.3166	.708919
11	9.0016	.684946
12	9.6633	.661783
13	10.3027	.639404
14	10.9205	.617782
15	11.5174	.596891
16	12.0941	.576706
17	12.6513	.557204
18	13.1897	.538361
19	13.7098	.520156
20	14.2124	.502566
21	14.6980	.485571
22	15.1671	.469151
23	15.6204	.453286
24	16.0584	.437957
25	16.4815	.423147
26	16.8904	.408838
27	17.2854	.395012
28	17.6670	.381654
29	18.0358	.368748
30	18.3920	.356278

FEDERAL ESTATE TAX REGULATIONS
EXPLAINING THE VALUATION OF

Annuities, Life Estates, Remainders, and Reversions

Below is given section 81.10(i) of the Federal estate tax Regulations, applicable to estates of persons dying after December 31, 1951. Similar rules for the Federal gift tax are contained in section 86.19(f) of the gift tax Regulations.

(1) *In general.* The value of an annuity contract, or an insurance policy on the life of a person other than the decedent, issued by a company regularly engaged in the selling of contracts of that character is established through the sale by that company of comparable contracts. See section 86.19(i) of Regulations 108, relating to the gift tax. As to insurance on the life of the decedent, see section 81.28. Except with respect to the aforementioned annuity contracts and insurance policies, the values of annuities, life estates, remainders, and reversions are to be computed by the methods hereinafter prescribed in this paragraph. The present worth of such an interest which is dependent upon the continuation of, or termination of the life of one person or upon a term-certain is to be computed with the use of Table I or Table II of this section. If the interest to be valued is dependent upon more than one life or there is a term-certain concurrent with one or more lives see subparagraph (5) of this paragraph. For the purpose of the computation, the age of a person is to be taken as the

age of that person at his nearest birthday. If the executor adopts the option set forth in section 811(j) see section 81.11.

(2) *Annuities.—(i) Payable annually at end of year.* If the annuity is payable annually at the end of each year during the life of an individual, the amount payable annually should be multiplied by the figure in column 2 of Table I opposite the number of years in column 1 nearest the age of the individual whose life measures the duration of the annuity, or if payable for a definite number of years the amount payable annually should be multiplied by the figure in column 2 of Table II opposite the number of years in column 1.

Example (1). The decedent received under the terms of his father's will an annuity of $10,000 a year payable annually for the life of his elder brother. At the time he died, an annual payment had just been made. The brother at the decedent's death was 40 years 8 months old. By reference to Table I, the figure in column 2 opposite 41 years, the number nearest to the brother's actual age, is found to be 17.6853. The present worth of the annuity at the date of the decedent's death is, therefore, $176,853 ($10,000 multiplied by 17.6853).

Example (2). The decedent was entitled to receive an annuity of $10,000 a year payable at the end of annual periods throughout a term-certain. At the time he died, an annual payment had just been made and five more annual payments were still to be made. By reference to Table II, it is found that the figure in column 2 opposite 5 years is 4.5151. The present worth of the annuity is, therefore, $45,151 ($10,000 multiplied by 4.5151).

(ii) *Payable at end of semiannual, quarterly, monthly, or weekly periods.* If the annuity is payable at the end of semiannual, quarterly, monthly, or weekly periods, the value should be determined by multiplying the aggregate amount to be paid within a year by the figure in column 2 of Table I opposite the number of years in column 1 nearest the actual age of the person whose life measures the duration of the annuity, or the figure in column 2 of Table II opposite the number of years the annuity is payable, as the case may be, and then multiplying the product by 1.0171 for weekly payments, by 1.0159 for monthly payments, by 1.0130 for quarterly payments, or by 1.0087 for semiannual payments.

Example. If, in example (1) given above under subdivision (i), the annuity is payable semiannually, the aggregate annual amount, $10,000, should be multiplied by the factor 17.6853, and the product multiplied by 1.0087. The present worth of the annuity at the date of death is, therefore, $178,391.62 ($10,000 x 17.6853 x 1.0087).

(iii) *Payable at beginning of annual, semiannual, quarterly, monthly, or weekly periods.* (A) If the first payment of an annuity for the life of an individual is to be paid at once, the value of the annuity is the sum of the first payment plus the present worth of a similar annuity, the first payment of which is not to be made until the end of the first period.

Example. The decedent was entitled to receive an annuity of $50 a month payable during the life of another. The decedent died on the day a payment was due. At the date of the decedent's death the person whose life measures the duration of the annuity was 50 years of age. The value of the annuity at the date of decedent's death is $50 plus the product of $50 x 12 x 14.8486 (see Table I) x 1.0159, of $9,100.82.

(B) If the first payment of an annuity for a definite number of years is to be paid at once, the applicable factor is the product of the factor shown in Table II multiplied by 1.0177 for weekly payments, by 1.0189 for monthly payments, by 1.0218 for quarterly payments, by 1.0262 for semiannual payments, or by 1.0350 for annual payments.

Example. The decedent was the beneficiary of an annuity of $50 a month. On the day a payment was due, the decedent died. There were 300 payments to be made, including the payment due. The value of the annuity as of the date of decedent's death is the product of $50 x 12 x 16.4815 (see Table II) x 1.0189, or $10,075.80.

(3) *Life estates and terms for years.* If the interest to be valued consists of the right of a person for his life, or for the life of another person, or for a term of years, either to receive the income of certain property or to use nonincome-producing property, the value of the interest is the value of the property less the present worth of the remainder computed as shown below under subparagraph (4) of this paragraph.

Example. The decedent was entitled to receive the income from a fund of $50,000 during the life of a person 31 years old. The value of the life estate is $50,000 less $14,466 (computed as shown in the example under subparagraph (4) of this paragraph), or $35,534.

(4) *Remainders or reversionary interests.* If the decedent had a remainder or a reversionary interest in property subject to the life estate of another, the present worth of such interest should be obtained by multiplying the value of the property by the figure in column 3 of Table I opposite the number of years nearest to the actual age of the life tenant. In case the remainder or reversion is to take effect at the end of a term of years Table II should be used.

Example. The decedent was entitled to receive property worth $50,000 upon the death of his elder brother, to whom the income for life had been bequeathed. The brother at the time of the decedent's death was 31 years 5 months old. By reference to Table I, it is found that the figure in column 3 opposite 31 years is 0.28932. The present worth of the remainder interest at the date of death is, therefore, $14,466 ($50,000 multiplied by 0.28932).

(5) *Actuarial computations by Bureau.* If the interest to be valued is dependent upon the continuation of, or termination of more than one life, or there is a term-certain concurrent with one or more lives a special factor is necessary. Such factor is to be computed upon the basis of the makehamized mortality table appearing as Table 38 of United States Life Tables and Actuarial Tables 1939–1941, published by the United States Department of Commerce, Bureau of the Census, and interest at the rate of 3½ per cent a year, compounded annually. Many such factors may be found in, or readily computed with the use of the tables contained in a pamphlet entitled "Actuarial Values for Estate and Gift Tax," which may be purchased from the Superintendent of Documents, United States Government Printing Office, Washington 25, D. C.; or a case requiring a special factor (provided the case is that of an actual decedent and not merely proposed or hypothetical) may be stated to the Commissioner who will furnish such factor. The request must be accompanied by a statement of the date of birth of each person, the duration of whose life may affect the value of the interest, and by copies of the relevant instruments.

How to Figure Your Gift Tax for Past Years

Chapter 12 shows how to compute your Federal gift tax for 1955. But some people are still interested in the rates and exemptions that were in force back in the 1930's. Why? Because they may have just discovered that they should have filed gift tax returns for those years but didn't.

Where a return has not been filed for a certain year, the year is still "open." That is, the government can still assess a tax for the year, if a tax is due. The regular statute of limitations doesn't protect the taxpayer if he hasn't filed a return. Interest and penalties can be collected too.

If you think you have neglected to file gift tax returns for any year, better see your lawyer. Meanwhile, you may want to make a rough estimate of your overdue taxes. Here is the information you need:

IN GENERAL

The basic structure of the gift tax hasn't changed since the present system was started in 1932. Only the rates and exemptions have changed. If you understand how the tax for current years is computed, therefore, you may not have a great deal of difficulty with the tax for the "old" years.

278

HOW THE RATES AND EXEMPTIONS CHANGED

Tax for 1932. (Only gifts made after June 6, 1932, are taxed.)
Annual exclusion: $5,000, but none for gifts of future interests.
Lifetime exemption: $50,000
Rates: Table A below

Tax for 1933: All exemptions and rates same as 1932.

Tax for 1934: All exemptions and rates same as 1932.

Tax for 1935:
Annual exclusion: $5,000, but none for gifts of future interests.
Lifetime exemption: $50,000
Rates: Table B below

Tax for 1936:
Annual exclusion: $5,000, but none for gifts of future interests.
Lifetime exemption: $40,000. If you used more than $40,000 in earlier years, you must "give back" to the government the excess. (Add it to your total net gifts for earlier years.)
Rates: Table C below

Tax for 1937: All exemptions and rates same as 1936.

Tax for 1938: All exemptions and rates same as 1936.

Tax for 1939:
Annual exclusion: $4,000, but none for gifts of future interests or for gifts in trust.

Lifetime exemption: $40,000 (See 1936).
Rates: Table C below

Tax for 1940:
Annual exclusion: $4,000, but none for gifts of future interests or for gifts in trust.
Lifetime exemption: $40,000 (See 1936).
Rates: Table C below, but increase the tax attributable to gifts after June 25 by 10 per cent.

Tax for 1941:
Annual exclusion: $4,000, but none for gifts of future interests or for gifts in trust.
Lifetime exemption: $40,000 (See 1936).
Rates: Table C below, but increase the tax by 10 per cent.

Tax for 1942:
Annual exclusion: $4,000, but none for gifts of future interests or for gifts in trust.
Lifetime exemption: $40,000 (See 1936).
Rates: Table D below

Tax for 1943:
Annual exclusion: $3,000, but none for gifts of future interests.
Lifetime exemption: $30,000. If you used more than $30,000 in earlier years, you must give back to the government the excess. Do this by adding the excess to your total net gifts for earlier years. (You may already have given back some of the excess between 1936 and 1942, after the exemption had been lowered from $50,000 to $40,000.)
Rates: Table D below

Tax for 1944 and later years: All exemptions and rates same as 1943.

THE GIFT TAX RATES FOR ALL YEARS

(You aren't interested in the old rates—Tables A, B, and C—if you are figuring your tax for 1957 or any other year after 1941. But if you have neglected to file returns for past years and are now estimating what you owe the government, you will want to figure the tax you should have paid for each year back as far as 1932. To do that you will need the old rates.)

TABLE A
(FOR AFTER JUNE 6, 1932; 1933; AND 1934)

(1) AMOUNT OF GIFTS (AFTER DEDUCTING ALL EXEMPTIONS, EXCLUSIONS, AND DEDUCTIONS)	(2) TAX ON AMOUNT IN COL. I	(3) RATE OF TAX ON NEXT BRACKET (PER CENT)
$ -o-	$ -o-	¾
10,000	75	1½
20,000	225	2¼
30,000	450	3
40,000	750	3¾
50,000	1,125	5
100,000	3,625	6½
200,000	10,125	8
400,000	26,125	9½
600,000	45,125	11
800,000	67,125	12½
1,000,000	92125	14
1,500,000	162,125	15½
2,000,000	239,625	17
2,500,000	324,625	18½
3,000,000	417,125	20
3,500,000	517,125	21½
4,000,000	624,625	23
4,500,000	739,625	24½
5,000,000	862,125	26
6,000,000	1,122,125	27½
7,000,000	1,397,125	29
8,000,000	1,687,125	30½
9,000,000	1,992,125	32
10,000,000	2,312,125	33½

TABLE B

(FOR 1935)

(1)	(2)	(3)
AMOUNT OF GIFTS (AFTER DEDUCTING ALL EXEMPTIONS, EXCLUSIONS, AND DEDUCTIONS)	TAX ON AMOUNT IN COL. I	RATE OF TAX ON NEXT BRACKET (PER CENT)
$ -o-	$ -o-	¾
10,000	75	1½
20,000	225	2¼
30,000	450	3
40,000	750	3¾
50,000	1,125	5¼
70,000	2,175	6¾
100,000	4,200	9
200,000	13,200	12
400,000	37,200	14¼
600,000	65,700	16½
800,000	98,700	18¾
1,000,000	136,200	21
1,500,000	241,200	23¼
2,000,000	357,450	25½
2,500,000	484,950	27¾
3,000,000	623,700	30
3,500,000	773,700	32¼
4,000,000	934,950	34½
4,500,000	1,107,450	36
5,000,000	1,287,450	37½
6,000,000	1,662,450	39
7,000,000	2,052,450	40½
8,000,000	2,457,450	42
9,000,000	2,877,450	43½
10,000,000	3,312,450	45

TABLE C

(FOR 1936, 1937, 1938, 1939, 1940, AND 1941. BUT FOR 1940 THE TAX
ATTRIBUTABLE TO GIFTS AFTER JUNE 25 SHOULD BE INCREASED BY 10
PER CENT; AND THE TAX FOR ALL OF 1941 SHOULD BE INCREASED BY
10 PER CENT.)

(1) AMOUNT OF GIFTS (AFTER DEDUCTING ALL EXEMPTIONS, EXCLUSIONS, AND DEDUCTIONS)	(2) TAX ON AMOUNT IN COL. 1	(3) RATE OF TAX ON NEXT BRACKET (PER CENT)
$ -o-	$ -o-	1½
10,000	150	3
20,000	450	4½
30,000	900	6
40,000	1,500	7½
50,000	2,250	9
70,000	4,050	10½
100,000	7,200	12¾
200,000	19,950	15
400,000	49,950	17¼
600,000	84,450	19½
800,000	123,450	21¾
1,000,000	166,950	24
1,500,000	286,950	26¼
2,000,000	418,200	28½
2,500,000	560,700	30¾
3,000,000	714,450	33
3,500,000	879,450	35¼
4,000,000	1,055,700	37½
4,500,000	1,243,200	39¾
5,000,000	1,441,950	42
6,000,000	1,861,950	44¼
7,000,000	2,304,450	45¾
8,000,000	2,761,950	47¼
9,000,000	3,234,450	48¾
10,000,000	3,721,950	50¼
20,000,000	8,746,950	51¾
50,000,000	24,271,950	52½

TABLE D

(FOR 1942 AND ALL LATER YEARS)

(1) AMOUNT OF GIFTS (AFTER DEDUCTING ALL EXEMPTIONS, EXCLUSIONS, AND DEDUCTIONS)	(2) TAX ON AMOUNT IN COL. I	(3) RATE OF TAX ON NEXT BRACKET (PER CENT)
$ -o-	$ -o-	2¼
5,000	112½	5¼
10,000	375	8¼
20,000	1,200	10½
30,000	2,250	13½
40,000	3,600	16½
50,000	5,250	18¾
60,000	7,125	21
100,000	15,525	22½
250,000	49,275	24
500,000	109,275	26¼
750,000	174,900	27¾
1,000,000	244,275	29¼
1,250,000	317,400	31½
1,500,000	396,150	33¾
2,000,000	564,900	36¾
2,500,000	748,650	39¾
3,000,000	947,400	42
3,500,000	1,157,400	44¼
4,000,000	1,378,650	47¼
5,000,000	1,851,150	50¼
6,000,000	2,353,650	52½
7,000,000	2,878,650	54¾
8,000,000	3,426,150	57
10,000,000	4,566,150	57¾

INTEREST AND PENALTIES

INTEREST: Generally, unpaid gift tax costs the taxpayer 6 per cent per year interest, from the date the tax was due until the date it is paid.

PENALTIES: There is a penalty of up to 25 per cent of the tax for failure to file a return on time.

There is a penalty of 5 per cent of tax deficiencies that are due to the taxpayer's negligence.

There are also severe penalties when the government can prove fraud with intent to evade the tax, or where there has been a willful attempt to evade tax.

How to Figure Estate Tax When the Amount of Tax and the Amount of a Deduction Are Interdependent

BY ALGEBRA

Let's say that a man is worth $200,000. In his will he directs that debts, expenses, and taxes be paid. Then he gives half of what's left to his wife and the other half to his children.

Assume the debts and expenses come to $20,000.

Assume the *State* inheritance or estate tax is $10,000.

In many of the States you can figure the State tax without knowing the amount of the Federal tax. That is because, in these States, the Federal tax is not allowed as a deduction in figuring the State tax. And you can be pretty sure, in many of the States, that the State tax will be more than the largest amount that can be credited against the Federal tax—especially in a situation where there is a large marital deduction for Federal tax but no corresponding deduction for the State tax.

There will be a marital deduction for the property going

to the wife. But we can't know how much that will be until
we know how much the Federal tax will be.

Now let's see what we do know:

The *gross estate* is	$200,000
The *debts and expenses* are	20,000
The *adjusted gross estate* is	180,000
The *State tax* is	10,000
The *Federal tax* is	X (unknown)
The *residue of the estate* is	170,000 — X
The amount going to the	
wife (the *marital deduction*) is	$\dfrac{170,000 - X}{2}$
The *exemption* is	60,000

The *net (or "taxable") estate* is

$$\$180,000 - \left(\frac{\$170,000 - X}{2}\right) - \$60,000$$

We also know the rates of tax against a net estate of any
given size (see pages 139–141).

The next thing we need to know is *about* how much X,
the Federal tax, is. Then we can know *about* how much the
marital deduction is and *about* how much the net estate is.

X can't be more than $25,820. That's the tax on $180,000
less a $60,000 exemption.

And X can't be less than $3,000. That's the tax you'd get
by taking off the largest possible marital deduction—$90,000.

So the marital deduction is somewhere between

$$\frac{\$170,000 - \$25,820}{2}, \text{ or } \$72,090$$

and

$$\frac{\$170,000 - \$3,000}{2}, \text{ or } \$83,500.$$

Therefore the net estate is somewhere between

$$\$180,000 - \$72,090 - \$60,000, \text{ or } \$47,910$$

and

$$\$180,000 - \$83,500 - \$60,000, \text{ or } \$36,500.$$

The net estate is probably much closer to the lower figure, $36,500, than to the higher, because surely there will be a large amount of property going to the wife and therefore a large marital deduction.

Let's make a guess. Guess that the net estate will be under $40,000.

Now look at the table of rates on page 139. What is the tax on a net (or "taxable") estate of

$$\$180,000 - \left. \frac{\$170,000 - X)}{2} \right) - \$60,000,$$

assuming that the above conglomeration of figures is something between $30,000 and $40,000?

It is:

$$\$3,000 \text{ (the tax on a \$30,000 net estate)}$$

$$+$$

$$18\% \text{ of the net estate less \$30,000.}$$

Write it this way:

$$X = \$3,000 + .18 \left[180,000 - \frac{170,000 - X}{2} - 60,000 - 30,000 \right]$$

Take our word for it, X, the Federal tax, comes out of that formula as $4,285.71.

So, if our guess was right:

the *Federal tax* is	$ 4,285.71
the *marital deduction* is	82,857.14
the *net (or "taxable") estate* is	37,142.86

Matching a $37,142.86 net ("taxable") estate against the rate table, you will find that the tax is $4,285.71. So it "proves."

There are some ready-made formulas for working out this problem. However, it may take you considerable time to adapt one of these formulas to your own particular problem. As an alternative, we suggest that you work out your own formula on the spot, as we have done in the preceding computation.

Do it this way:

Write down what you know about the estate—the gross estate, the deductions for debts and expenses, the State tax, and so forth.

For the Federal tax, put down X.

Then proceed to express the net, or "taxable," estate in terms of X.

Finally, make a guess as to which bracket of the tax scale the net estate comes within. If you think carefully about it, you'll guess right nearly every time.

From that point on it's clear sailing. X, the Federal tax, is the tax on the lowest amount in the bracket plus the applicable rate on the amount by which the net estate (expressed in terms of X) exceeds that lowest amount.

If you have an estate where the State tax also is unknown —where the Federal tax, for instance, is an allowable deduction in figuring the State tax—the problem is harder.

Call the Federal tax X and the State tax Y. Write down what Y is in terms of X. For example, Y might be

$$\$1,500 + 4\% \ (\$170,000 - X - 150,000)$$

Then find X in terms of Y. For example, you might find that X is $4,500—.18Y.

Then go back and find out how much Y is in dollars and cents by substituting the answer for X in the first equation.

It's complicated. But it can always be worked out and you can prove your answer.

BY MAGIC TABLES

First problem: A husband's will says (in the proper legal language):

"I want my executor to pay my debts, the expenses of settling my estate, and all my estate and inheritance taxes. What's left is to go half to my wife and half to my children."

The amount going to the wife is a marital deduction, so the Federal tax cannot be figured until you know how much she receives. But the amount she receives cannot be known until the amount of Federal tax is known.

Solution: Suppose the gross estate is $220,000. The debts and expenses are $20,000. That brings the estate down to $200,000.

The State tax, we'll say, is $6,050. Deduct it from the $200,000. That leaves $193,950 *less the Federal tax* to be divided between the wife and children.

To find the Federal tax—
  (1) take half of $193,950 $96,975.00
      (Call this the "unadjusted marital deduction.")
  (2) deduct it from $200,000 $103,025.00
      (Call this the "unadjusted taxable estate.")
  (3) find the tax on $103,025 from Table A $6,086.46
      (This is your answer. It is the Federal tax re-
      duced by the maximum credit for State tax.)

TABLE A

(A) UNADJUSTED TAXABLE ESTATE	(B) TAX ON AMOUNT IN COL. (A)	(C) RATE ON NEXT BRACKET (PER CENT)
$ 60,000	$ –0–	3.04569
64,925	150	7.25389
69,750	500	11.64021
79,200	1,600	15.05376
88,500	3,000	19.78022
97,600	4,800	23.71365
106,540	6,920	27.53129
115,330	9,340	31.48148
141,250	17,500	30.41475
149,930	20,140	33.10023
184,250	31,500	32.01856
270,450	59,100	30.94688
279,110	61,780	33.64486
441,750	116,500	32.55814
493,350	133,300	36.68639
611,650	176,700	35.57126
705,040	209,920	38.37902
780,550	238,900	37.24792
915,430	289,140	40.90604
948,750	302,500	38.94863
1,124,520	370,960	43.30900
1,330,020	459,960	47.83147
1,362,300	475,400	46.60912
1,735,360	649,280	52.84450
1,767,000	666,000	51.57233
2,132,700	854,600	

Calculations by Kennedy Sinclaire, Inc., 140 Cedar Street, New York, N. Y.

SECOND PROBLEM: What if ALL the Federal tax comes out of the share going to the wife? For example, a husband's will provides:

Debts and expenses are to be paid; then a $350,000 general legacy in trust for the wife (trust does not qualify for the marital deduction); then residue outright to wife, with all taxes payable out of residue.

SOLUTION: Suppose the estate, after debts and expenses, is $700,000. After the trust is set up there is $350,000 left. The State tax, say, is $34,550. That leaves $315,450 *less the Federal tax* for the wife.

To find the Federal tax—

    (1) take all of the $315,450 $315,450.00
        (Call this the "unadjusted marital deduction.")

    (2) deduct it from $700,000 $384,550.00
        (Call this the "unadjusted taxable estate.")

    (3) find the tax on $384,550 from Table B $116,908.33
        (This is your answer. It is the Federal tax reduced by the maximum credit for State tax.)

TABLE B

(A) UNADJUSTED TAXABLE ESTATE	(B) TAX ON AMOUNT IN COL. (A)	(C) RATE ON NEXT BRACKET (PER CENT)
$ 60,000	$ –0–	3.09278
64,850	150	7.52688
69,500	500	12.35955
78,400	1,600	16.27907
87,000	3,000	21.95122
95,200	4,800	26.90355
103,080	6,920	31.92612
110,660	9,340	37.36264
132,500	17,500	35.86957
139,860	20,140	39.66480
168,500	31,500	38.12155
240,900	59,100	36.61202
248,220	61,780	40.44944
383,500	116,500	38.88889
426,700	133,300	44.92754
523,300	176,700	43.26648
600,080	209,920	47.49263
661,100	238,900	45.77259
770,860	289,140	50.15015
797,500	302,500	48.36795
939,040	370,960	55.27950
1,100,040	459,960	62.86645
1,124,600	475,400	60.77170
1,410,720	649,280	71.82130
1,434,000	666,000	69.49153
1,705,400	854,600	

Calculations by Kennedy Sinclaire, Inc., 140 Cedar Street, New York, N. Y.

Valuation of Closely Held Stock

Below is given Revenue Ruling 54-77, IRB 1954-9.

SECTION I. PURPOSE

The purpose of this revenue ruling is to outline and review in general the approach, methods and factors to be considered in valuing shares of the capital stock of closely held corporations for estate and gift tax purposes. The methods discussed herein will apply likewise to the valuation or corporate stocks on which market quotations are either unavailable or are of such scarcity that they do not reflect the fair market value.

SEC. 2. BACKGROUND AND DEFINITIONS.

.01 All valuations must be made in accordance with the applicable provisions of the Internal Revenue Code and the Federal estate tax and gift tax regulations. Sections 811 and 1005 of the Code require that the property to be included in the gross estate, or made the subject of gift, shall be taxed on the basis of the value of the property at the time of the death of the decedent, the optional date if so elected, or the date of gift.

.02 Section 81.10 of Estate Tax Regulations 105 and section 86.19 of Gift Tax Regulations 108 define fair market value, in effect, as the price at which the property would change hands between a willing buyer and a willing seller when the former is not under any compulsion to buy and the latter is not under any compulsion to sell. Court decisions frequently state in addition that the hypothetical buyer and seller are assumed to be able, as well as willing, to trade and to be well informed about the property and concerning the market for such property.

.03 Closely held corporations are those corporations the shares of which are owned by a relatively limited number of stockholders. Often the entire stock issue is held by one family. The result of this situation is that little, if any, trading in the shares takes place. There is, therefore, no established market for the stock and such sales as occur at irregular intervals seldom reflect all of the elements of a representative transaction as defined by the term "fair market value."

SEC. 3. APPROACH TO VALUATION

.01 Determination of fair market value, being a question of fact, will depend upon the circumstances in each case. No formula can be devised that will be generally applicable to the multitude of different valuation issues arising in estate and gift tax cases. Often an appraiser will find wide differences of opinion as to the fair market value of a particular stock. In resolving such differences he should maintain a reasonable attitude in recognition of the fact that valuation is not an exact science. A sound valuation will be based upon all the relevant facts, but the elements of common sense, informed judgment and reasonableness must enter into the process of weighing those facts and determining their aggregate significance.

.02 The fair market value of a specific property will vary as general economic conditions change from "normal" to "boom" or "depression"; that is, according to the degree of optimism or pessimism with which the investing public regards the future at the required date of appraisal. Uncertainty as to the stability or continuity of the future income from a property decreases its value by increasing the risk of loss of earnings and value in the future. The value of a property with very uncertain future prospects is highly speculative. The appraiser must exercise his judgment as to the degree of risk attaching to a specific property, but that judgment must be related to all of the other factors affecting value.

SEC. 4. FACTORS TO CONSIDER.

.01 It is advisable to emphasize that in the valuation of the stock of closely held corporations or the stock of corporations where market quotations are either lacking or too scarce to be recognized, all available financial data, as well as all relevant factors affecting the fair market value, should be considered. The following factors, although not all-inclusive, are fundamental and require careful analysis in each case:

(a) The nature of the business and the history of the enterprise including the date of incorporation.

(b) The economic outlook in general and the condition and outcome of the specific industry in particular.

(c) The book value of the stock and the financial condition of the business.

(d) The earning capacity of the company.

(e) The dividend-paying capacity.

(f) Goodwill.

(g) Sales of the stock and the size of the block of stock to be valued.

(h) The market price of stocks of corporations engaged in the same or a similar line of business which are listed on an exchange.

.02 A brief discussion of each of the foregoing factors follows:

(a) The history of a corporate enterprise will show its past stability or instability, its growth or lack of growth, the diversity or lack of diversity of its operations, and other facts needed to form an opinion of the degree of risk involved in the business. For recently incorporated companies the history of predecessor businesses should be considered. The detail to be considered should increase with approach to the required date of appraisal, since recent events are of greatest help in predicting the future; but a study of gross and net income, and of dividends covering a long prior period, is highly desirable. The history to be studied should include, but need not be limited to, the nature of the business, its products or services, its operating and investment assets, capital structure, plant facilities and management, all of which should be considered as of the date of the appraisal, with due regard for recent significant changes. Events of the past that are unlikely to recur in the future should be discounted, since value has a close relation to future expectancy.

(b) A sound appraisal of a closely held stock must consider current and prospective economic conditions as of the date of appraisal, both in the national economy and in the industry or industries with which the corporation is allied. It is important to know that the company is more, or less, successful than its competitors in the same industry, or that it is maintaining a stable position with respect to competitors. Equal or even greater significance may attach to the ability of the industry with which the company is allied to compete with other industries. Prospective competition which has not been a factor in prior years should be given careful attention. The public's appraisal of the future prospects of competitive industries or of competitors within an industry may be indicated by price trends in the markets for commodities and for securities. The death of the manager of a so-called "one-man" business may have a depressing effect upon the value of the stock of such business, particularly if there is a lack of trained personnel capable of succeeding to the management of the enterprise. In valuing the stock of this type of business, therefore, the effect of the loss of the manager on the future expectancy of the business, and the absence of management-succession potentialities are pertinent factors to be taken into consideration. On the other hand, there may be factors which offset, in whole or in part, the loss of the manager's services. For instance, the nature of the business and of its assets may be such that they will not be impaired by the death of the manager. Furthermore, the loss may be adequately covered by life insurance, or competent management might be employed on the basis of the consideration paid for the former manager's services. These, or other offsetting factors, if found to exist, should be carefully weighed against the loss of the manager's services in valuing the stock of the enterprise.

(c) Balance sheets should be obtained, preferably in the form of comparative annual statements for two or more years immediately preceding the date of appraisal, together with a balance sheet at the end of the month preceding that date, if corporate accounting will permit. Any balance sheet descriptions that are not self-explanatory, and balance sheet items comprehending diverse assets or liabilities, should be clarified in essential detail by obtaining supplemental schedules. These statements usually will disclose to the appraiser, (1) liquid position (ratio of current assets to liabilities); (2) amount of net fixed assets; (3) working capital; (4) long-term indebtedness; (5) capital structure; and (6) net worth. Consideration also should be given to any assets not essential to the operation of the business, such as investments in securities, real estate, etc. In general, such nonoperating assets will command a lower rate of return than do the operating assets, although in exceptional cases the reverse may be true. In computing the book value per share of stock, assets of the investment type should be revalued on the basis of their market price and the book value adjusted accordingly. Comparison of the company's balance sheets over several years may reveal, among other facts, such developments as the acquisition of additional production facilities or subsidiary companies, improvement in financial position, and details as to recapitalizations and other changes in the capital structure of the corporation. If the corporation has more than one class of stock outstanding, the charter or certificate of incorporation should be examined to ascertain the explicit rights and privileges of the various stock issues including: (1) voting power, (2) preference as to dividends, and (3) preference as to assets in the event of liquidation.

(d) Detailed profit-and-loss statements should be obtained and considered for a representative period immediately prior to the required date of appraisal, preferably five or more years. Such statements should show (1) gross income by principal items; (2) principal deductions from gross income including major prior items of operating expense, interest and other expense on each item of long-term debt, depreciation and depletion if such deductions are made, officers' salaries in total if they appear to be reasonable or in detail if they seem to be excessive, contributions (whether or not deductible for tax purposes) that the nature of its business and its community position require the corporation to make, and taxes by principal items, including income and excess-profits taxes; (3) net income available for dividends; (4) rates and amounts of dividends paid on each class of stock; (5) remaining amount carried to surplus; and (6) adjustments to, and reconciliation with, surplus as stated on the balance sheet. With profit and loss statements of this character available, the appraiser should be able to separate recurrent from nonrecurrent items of income and expense, to distinguish between operating income and investment income, and to ascertain whether or not any line of business in which the company is engaged is operated consistently at a loss and might be abandoned with benefit to the company. The percentage of earnings retained for business expansion should be noted when dividend-paying capacity is considered. Potential future income is a major factor in many valuations of closely held stocks, and all information concerning past income which will be helpful in predicting the future should be secured. Prior earnings records usually are the most reliable guide as to future expectancy, but resort to arbitrary five-or-ten-year averages without regard to current trends or future prospects will not produce a realistic valuation. If, for instance, a record of progressively increasing or decreasing net income is found, then greater weight may be accorded the most recent years' profits in estimating earning power. It will be helpful, in judging risk and the extent to which a business is a marginal operator, to consider deductions from income and net income in terms of percentage of sales. Major categories of cost and expense to be so analyzed include the consumption of raw materials and supplies in the case of manufacturers, processors and fabricators; the cost of purchased merchandise in the case of merchants; utility services; insurance; taxes; depletion or depreciation; and interest.

(e) Primary consideration should be given to the dividend-paying capacity of the company rather than to dividends actually paid in the past. Dividend-paying capacity is a factor that must be considered in an appraisal, but dividends actually paid in the past may not have any relation to dividend-paying capacity. Specifically, the dividends paid by a closely held family company may be measured by the income needs of the stockholders or by their desire to avoid taxes on dividend receipts, instead of by ability of the company to pay dividends. Where an actual or effective controlling interest in a corporation is to be valued, the dividend factor is not a material element, since the payment of such dividends is discretionary with the controlling stockholders. The individual or group in control can substitute salaries and bonuses for dividends, thus reducing net income and understating the dividend-paying capacity of the company. It follows, therefore, that dividends are less reliable criteria of fair market value than other applicable factors.

(f) In the final analysis, goodwill is based upon earning capacity. The presence of goodwill and its value, therefore, rests upon the excess of net earnings over and above a fair return on the net tangible assets. Such excess earnings capitalized at an appropriate rate will furnish one basis on which to value the goodwill applicable to the stock, but not necessarily the controlling basis. While the element of goodwill may be based primarily on earnings, such factors as the prestige and renown of the business, the ownership of a trade or brand name, and a record of successful operation over a prolonged period in a particular locality, also may furnish support for the inclusion of intangible value.

(g) Sales of stock of a closely held corporation should be carefully investigated to determine whether they represent transactions at arm's length. Forced or distress sales do not ordinarily reflect fair market value, nor do isolated sales in small amounts necessarily control as the measure of value. This is especially true in the valuation of a controlling interest in a corporation. Since, in the case of closely held stocks, no prevailing market prices are available, there is no basis for making an adjustment for blockage. It follows, therefore, that such stocks should be valued upon a consideration of all the evidence affecting the fair market value. The size of the block of stock itself is a relevant factor to be considered. Although it is true that a minority interest in an unlisted corporation's stock is more difficult to sell than a similar block of listed stock, it is equally true that control of a corporation, either actual or effective, representing as it does an added element of value, may justify a higher value for a specific block of stock.

(h) The Revenue Act of 1943 amended the Internal Revenue Code by adding subsection (k) of section 811, which states, in effect, that in valuing unlisted securities the value of listed stocks or securities of corporations engaged in the same or similar line of business should be taken into consideration. In selecting corporations for comparative purposes, care should be taken to use only truly comparable companies. For illustration, a corporation having one or more issues of preferred stock, bonds or debentures in addition to its common stock should not be considered comparable to one having only commn stock outstanding. In like manner, a company with declining business and contracting markets is not comparable to one with a record of current progress and market expansion. The test should be for similarity not only of the type of business but of the trend of earnings, capital structure, volume of sales, and size in terms of total assets, as well, in order that the most valid comparison possible will be obtained.

SEC. 5. WEIGHT TO BE ACCORDED VARIOUS FACTORS.

The valuation of closely held corporate stock entails the consideration of all relevant factors as stated in section 4. Depending upon the circumstances in each case, certain factors may carry more weight than others because of the nature of the company's business. To illustrate:

(a) Earnings may be the most important criterion of value in some cases whereas asset value will receive primary consideration in others. In general the appraiser will accord primary consideration to earnings when valuing stocks of companies which sell products or services to the public; conversely, in the investment or holding type of company, the appraiser may accord the greatest weight to the assets underlying the security to be valued.

(b) The value of the stock of a personal or family holding company is closely related to the value of the assets underlying the stock. For companies of this type the appraiser should determine the fair market values of the assets of the company. Operating expenses of the holding company and cost of liquidating it, if any, merit consideration when appraising the relative values of the stock and of the underlying assets. The market values of the underlying assets give due weight to potential earnings and dividends of the particular items of property underlying the stock, capitalized at rates deemed proper by the investing public at the date of appraisal. A current appraisal by the investing public should be superior to the retrospective opinion of an individual. For these reasons adjusted net worth should be accorded greater weight in valuing the stock of a closely held family or personal holding company than any of the other customary yardsticks of appraisal, such as earnings and dividend paying capacity.

SEC. 6. CAPITALIZATION RATES.

In the application of certain fundamental valuation factors, such as earnings and dividends, it is necessary to capitalize the average or current results at some appropriate rate. Determination of the proper capitalization rate presents one of the most difficult problems in valuation. That there is no ready or simple solution will be made apparent by a cursory check of the rates of return and dividend yields in terms of the selling prices of corporate shares listed on the major exchanges of the country. Wide variations will be found even for companies in the same industry. Moreover the ratio will fluctuate from year to year depending upon economic conditions. Thus, no standard tables of capitalization rates applicable to closely held corporations can be formulated. Among the more important factors to take into consideration in deciding upon a capitalization rate in a particular case are: (1) the nature of the business; (2) the risk involved; and (3) the stability or irregularity of earnings.

SEC. 7. AVERAGE OF FACTORS.

Because valuations cannot be made on the basis of a prescribed formula, there is no means whereby the various applicable factors in a particular case can be assigned mathematical weights in deriving the fair market value. For this reason no useful purpose is served by taking an average of several factors (for example: book value, capitalized earnings and capitalized dividends) and basing the valuation on the result. Such a process excludes active consideration of other pertinent factors, and the end result is incapable of being supported by a realistic application of the significant facts in the case except by mere chance.

SEC. 8. RESTRICTIVE AGREEMENTS.

Frequently, in the valuation of closely held stock for estate and gift tax purposes, it will be found that the stock is subject to an agreement restricting its sale or transfer. Where shares of stock were acquired by a decedent subject to an option reserved by the issuing corporation to repurchase at a certain price, the option price is usually accepted as the fair market value for estate tax purposes. See Rev. Rul. 54-76 below. However, in such case the option price is not determinative of fair market value for gift tax purposes. Where the option, or buy and sell agreement, is the result of voluntary action by the stockholders and is binding during the life as well as at the death of the stockholders, such agreement may or may not, depending upon the circumstances of each case, fix the value for estate tax purposes. However, such agreement is a factor to be considered, with other relevant factors, in determining fair market value. Where the stockholder is free to dispose of his shares during life and the option is to become effective only upon his death, the fair market value is not limited to the option price. It is always necessary to consider the relationship of the parties, the relative number of shares held by the decedent, and other material facts, to determine whether the agreement represents a bona fide business arrangement or is a device to pass the decedent's shares to the natural objects of his bounty for less than an adequate and full consideration in money or money's worth. In this connection see Rev. Rul. 157, IRB 1953-17, 16 and Rev. Rul. 189, IRB 1953-19, 19.

Index